LEVEL UP

Level Up

Time to Motivate your Faith

Carolyn A. Roth

CRM Publishing

Level Up, *Time to motivate your faith.*

Published in the United States of America
Publisher: CRM (Carolyn Roth Ministry) Publishing

978-1-946919-17-5
Religion and Spirituality
Religious Studies
Psychology and Christianity
24-08-30

DEDICATION

my brother and sister,

Roger and Julie

I'm just a nobody trying to tell everybody about somebody who saved my soul.

--Casting Crowns, source LyricFind

ACKNOWLEDGEMENTS

A huge thank you to my husband, Bruce Roth, editor and supporter extraordinaire.

Thank you for my superlative girlfriends.

CONTENTS

IT'S JUST BEGUN

Every individual living in the 21ˢᵗ century is a product of God's judgment in the Garden of Eden. Between Adam and Eve's sin and the 21ˢᵗ century, humankind experienced the consequences of sin.

God initiated rescue plans to free humans from the consequences of Adam and Eve's disobedience. God's first plan was centered around the Tabernacle and focused on the Israelites. Later (1500-2000 years) God initiated a better plan. That plan is open to all humankind, not just a single tribe (Israelites). God's current rescue plan occurs through belief in God's Son (Jesus, the Christ) as Savior. At the end of the ages, individuals who have a relationship with Jesus as Savior will be with God. Others won't be.

Christians toil to live a Jesus-centered life. This book is for those Christians who want help with day-to-day living. The book's overall purpose is to show 21st-century Christians how to level up their Christian walk by applying stories from the Bible.

The book has two objectives. The first is to take a deep dive into Bible episodes. Bible stories show characters' efforts to walk with God. Some efforts succeeded. Some failed. All teach us. God expects Christians to know and learn from Bible stories. That's why they're in the Bible.

The book's second objective is to apply the outcomes of Bible episodes to our efforts to live a more successful Christian life in the 21st century.

Leveling up our Christian walk doesn't sound all that hard. Possibly, you asked, "Do I really need this book? How is it different from a thousand other books on the market?"

The book is different because it integrates Bible (the Christian's self-help book) instruction with the latest information on how to make behavioral changes. Further, instructions are documented with biblical references, lots and lots of Bible references.

The book engages and stimulates your thinking. Chapters incorporate thought-provoking questions throughout. Questions require you to take an in-depth look at how you live your life. You decide if you want to go in your current direction. Alternatively, is it time to make a directional change? Do you need a course correction? I've already gone through the process outlined in this book. It isn't quick or easy. Maybe, I'll go through it a few more times.

Each chapter's final page is "Delving Deeper." Delving Deeper is filled with questions that encourage you to take a deeper dive into Holy Scripture. Then, deliberate on what you believe and, importantly, why you believe it. Questions are ideally suited for single persons or groups

Chapter 1

HIGH HOPES

"High Hope" is a catchy tune with uplifting lyrics.[1] The song is a message of resilience, optimism, and the power of dreaming big. The song encourages us to pursue our goals, even if the odds of achieving them are against us. It tells us that with hard work, determination, and a positive attitude, we can achieve anything we set our minds to.

God had high hopes when he created humankind, a man and a woman. He wanted everything perfect for them, so he crafted a luscious garden, the Garden of Eden (delight), as their home. God told Adam to cultivate and tend the Garden. Likewise, we must cultivate and tend our lives. In the 21st century, cultivating a Christian life is challenging, sometimes even grueling. Nevertheless, we live with high hopes (a firm belief) in God's assistance.

In the 21st century, life is complicated, messy, and even chaotic. How did we get here? Life didn't start this way. It started in a serene garden where harmony abounded. Here's the story of how we moved from harmony to chaos.

Two creation stories are recorded in Genesis. In the first, God made the cosmos, Earth, and everything on and in it, including plants and trees, animals, birds, etc. Then, God decided to make humankind. Humankind was to rule over creatures on Earth, i.e., birds, animals, and fish. God created a male and a female (Genesis 1:27). God told them to multiply and fill the Earth.

In the second creation story (Genesis chapter 2), more details are given, such as:

- God created a man, then placed him in the Garden of Eden.
- God told the man not to eat from the Tree of Knowledge of Good and Evil in the center of the garden.
- God brought all animals to the man to name.
- Although each animal had a mate, the man didn't have one.
- God created a woman from the rib of the man to be his mate.
- The man was ecstatic when he saw his mate.

Have you ever wondered why there are two creation stories? Perhaps, they were told or written from two perspectives, just as there are four gospel perspectives on Jesus' life and teachings each written by a different person.

What would trigger you to give up home in a sumptuous Garden like Eden?

The man and woman lived in the Garden of Eden. His name was Adam; hers was Eve. Originally, nothing in the Garden, i.e., animals, plants, caused harm to Adam or Eve. God cared for and communicated with them.

All of God's creation was in harmony; there was no discord, dissension, or conflict. Similarly, nothing in Genesis chapters 1 and 2 indicates that Eve was Adam's subordinate.

****

The harmony and equality in Adam and Eve's relationship changed beginning in Genesis chapter three in a story named "The Fall." That change continued throughout the Bible and into the 21st century, yet it wasn't part of God's original plan when he created humankind.

Although many plants grew in the Garden of Eden, God named only two: the Tree of Life and the Tree of Knowledge of Good and Evil. God told Adam not to eat from the Tree of Knowledge of Good and Evil. Notice the name of the tree has to do with knowledge. The tree wasn't evil or bad, nor was the fruit it produced.

God told Adam that when he ate from the Tree of Knowledge of Good and Evil, Adam would die. Adam understood what death meant. His body would cease to be alive. God wouldn't have given Adam such a crucial command unless God was sure Adam understood it fully.

The words God used in Genesis (2:17) are noteworthy. God declared: *when,* not *if,* you eat from the Tree of Knowledge of Good and Evil, you will die. "When" means in the time that something is done or comes about. Even when God forbid Adam from eating Tree of Knowledge-fruit, God knew Adam would disobey him.

Adam knew which tree God meant when God said the Tree of Knowledge of Good and Evil. The tree was located near the center of Eden and produced fruit that looked good to eat. When God questioned Adam and Eve after they ate from the Tree of Knowledge of Good and Evil, neither responded with, "I didn't know which tree you meant."

Have you wondered why God placed a tree with attractive fruit in Eden, then warned Adam not to eat from it? Sounds mean, or even passive-aggressive, on God's part. The reason was related to Adam and Eve's free will. God wanted Adam and Eve to obey him willingly. God didn't want his highest creation to be robots who couldn't think for themselves. In the 21st century, a parallel is parents wanting their children to obey them out of love.

With their freewill, Adam and Eve rebelled against God's command not to eat from the Tree of

Knowledge of Good and Evil. They disobeyed God. That disobedience/rebellion is named "Sin."

In a macro sense, sin isn't an act or a series of acts. Sin is a condition that all of us are stuck in. No amount of human effort between Adam and Eve's era and the 21st century stopped humankind from sinning against God's commands. We are sinners, full stop! Most of us sin daily.

Does God give humans commands that they are unable to obey?

Humans are attracted to the forbidden. They want to do what they're told not to do. Ask any five-year-old! This child never thought about doing something before a parent or adult told him not to do it. Even as adults, we weigh forbidden acts. On a late evening, I sat at a traffic light. The light was red. I just finished working an evening shift at a hospital. I was tired and wanted to get home to bed. No cars were coming. I was tempted to take off and drive through that red light even though traffic laws forbid me to do so.

Why is the forbidden so attractive? We can't get it out of our mind.

****

When humankind disobeyed God's direct command not to eat fruit from the Tree of Knowledge, God didn't declare his creation "not good;" however, Adam and Eve's rebellion resulted in consequences.

Eating from the Tree of Knowledge of Good and Evil allowed Adam and Eve to make moral-ethical choices. 21st-century individuals make these types of choices every day. Moral-ethical choices are about right and wrong. They include treating others with respect, doing good, and acting justly.

Adam and Eve came from the hand of God. Initially, they possessed God's moral knowledge and perspective of right and wrong. But, after rebelling against God, they became morally corrupt (unethical, dishonest, tainted). That moral corruption extended through millennia into the 21st century. Today, you and I are morally corrupt without Jesus.

Being morally corrupt isn't God's will for us. God is good, holy, and loving; therefore, his plans and purposes for creation and his creatures are good, holy, and loving. As Ruler of the universe, God can and sometimes does send misfortune to accomplish his will. For example, God brought disaster to the Earth in the time of Noah. Today, God sends harmful weather patterns to get our attention and to discipline us. In the southeastern United States, we just experienced a Category 4 hurricane. Up to one million people were without electricity. Think of the misery of their lives with the high heat and humidity until electricity is restored.

In contrast to God's standards of morality, human standards are finite and flawed. They change as society's values change. Today, some individuals say that God's moral laws have changed since Eden. God adjusted, adjusts, and will adjust in the future what he names right or wrong as mankind's conscience evolves. That is a human-centric view that discounts Holy Scriptures which asserted that both God and his purpose are unchangeable (Malachi 3:6; Hebrews 6:16-17).

Where do your morals and ethics come from?

Only when our moral-ethical thoughts mirror God's are they accurate; however, you and I are marred by sin. Our thoughts, words, and actions degenerated from those of the perfect, sin-free beings God created.

When our human parents were created, they could choose to obey or disobey God. While they obeyed God, their lives were comfortable, pain-free, even serene. Has your life in the 21st century ever been serene? Probably not. What happened next in Genesis tells you why.

****

When Adam and Eve disobeyed God and ate fruit from the Tree of Knowledge of Good and Evil. everything changed. Adam and Eve lost their sinless state, their innocence. Then, they experienced the consequences of their rebellion.

Several consequences occurred. The first described in the Bible was that Adam and Eve became aware that they were naked. Adam was embarrassed for Eve to see his naked body. Likewise, Eve was embarrassed for Adam to see her body. To hide their nakedness, Adam and Eve sewed

23

fig leaves together and made aprons to cover themselves.

Despite Adam and Eve's disobedience against God's direction, God came searching for them. Think about that! God came searching for Adam and Eve, even though God knew they disobeyed him. God called out to Adam and Eve; God calls out to you and me.

In God's presence, Adam blurted out that he hid because he was naked. In reality, Adam wasn't naked. He wore a fig leaf apron. In Adam's mind, the fig leaf apron was adequate to cover his nakedness in front of Eve, but not in front of God.

As God searched for Adam and Eve, God searches for us.

Wearing clothes began in the Garden of Eden with an act of disobedience to God's command. Today, wearing clothes is the norm. We dress for the day soon after getting out of bed. I don't know about you, but I want to look good to others. I want to present myself as a person who is attractive physically, psychologically, and spiritually. Yet, I'm not always like that.

Worse than projecting an idealized picture of myself to others, I try to project this picture to God. Do you ever disobey God and then lie to God about it? I do! I attempt to obscure my true motives before God, even spin them so that I look good.

What an amazing waste of time! God knew me before the Earth was created and when I was in my mother's womb. He knows the number of hairs on my head. God knows my true motives. God knows when I attempt to put something over on my boss, my spouse, or him.

****

After rebelling against God, Adam was no longer the caretaker of a sumptuous garden and its produce. He and Eve were expelled from the Garden of Eden. Henceforth, Adam toiled (worked, sweated) to raise vegetables and grow fruit to feed his family. Thorns began to grow on trees. Thistles grew in fields. As Adam and his offspring plowed and planted crops, some native plants became weeds which made farming difficult.

When Adam heard God say that going forward the land would produce thorns and thistles, Adam couldn't relate to that consequence. Adam had no experience with thorns and thistles. In the Garden of Eden, no plants had structures—spines, prickles, thorns—that damaged humans' skin. Likely, Adam thought this part of God's punishment wasn't all that bad.

Possibly, the first time Eve encountered a thorn was while selecting fruit from a tree. The thorn pierced and scratched her arm. Maybe, blood appeared. It hurt. Likely, Eve asked, "What is this thing growing on the tree that stabbed me?" Eve showed her injury to Adam and told him to be careful not to get stabbed by that tree.

One rarely mentioned consequence of Adam and Eve's disobedience was pain. In the 21st century, pain occurs in both males and females. The Bible identified only the pain of childbirth (Genesis 3:16, John 16:21). In the 21st century, some women don't give birth to children, but all women have pain. Men aren't exempt from pain.

Do you know anyone who never experienced pain?

Most pain is physical. Physical pain results from something as minor as a pulled muscle, sprained tendon, or food moving through the digestive tract. Physical pain occurs when individuals are in car accidents or have debilitating diseases. During war, servicemen and women experience pain from bullets, knives, or bombs. Noncombatants are intentionally or unintentionally harmed in a war environment.

Emotional pain causes tremendous suffering. Emotional pain can be worse than physical pain. There's little medication to relieve it. Emotional pain stems from disappointment, fear, betrayal, and guilt. Often, we replay painful events in our minds. Our chest hurts, bowels cease to work, and head aches. Sometimes, emotional pain leads to depression, which worsens emotional pain.

I dislike pain. Humans dislike pain, all types of pain. We do our best to avoid it. Yet, when we disobey God, we suffer consequences that often include physical or emotional pain.

At one time, I thought that if I confessed my sin, I no longer had to experience its consequences. Wrong! Wrong! Wrong! Adam and Eve were aware that they had rebelled (sinned) against God's direction. Perhaps, they even told God they were

26

sorry. Nonetheless, they, like us, had to experience the consequences of their sin.

The question for Christians today is, "How can we avoid disobeying God when we live in a busy, complex society? There are many answers proposed by psychologists, but I like the one that came from Brother Lawrence.[2] Brother Lawrence (1614–1691 CE) was a monk and the monastery cook. Brother Lawrence practiced thinking about God while cooking, cleaning, etc.

Eventually, Brother Lawrence's intentional awareness of God became a habit of living in God's presence, which reduced sin and the consequences of sin in his life. Have you reached the point in your life that you are consumed by thoughts of God while cooking, doing housework, or mowing the lawn?

****

Why did God allow Adam and Eve to eat from the Tree of Life but not the Tree of Knowledge?

Although God told Adam and Eve that they couldn't eat from the Tree of Knowledge of Good and Evil, God gave them no prohibition against eating fruit from the Tree of Life. Likely, they ate Tree-of-Life-fruit while living in the Garden of Eden.

Adam and Eve's access to the Tree of Life depended on a proper relationship with God. When the relationship was severed, so was their access to the life-giving tree.

Do you have a Spirit-filled life, or are you just trudging along?

After Adam and Eve ate from the Tree of Knowledge of Good and Evil, God reflected on their newfound knowledge:

> And the Lord God said, "The man has now become like one of us, knowing good and evil. He must not be allowed to reach out his hand and take also from the tree of life and eat, and live forever." So the Lord God banished him from the Garden of Eden to work the ground from which he had been taken. After he drove the man out, he placed cherubim on the east side of the Garden of Eden cherubim and a flaming sword flashing back and forth to guard the way to the tree of life (Genesis 3:22-24).

Not being able to eat from the Tree of Life meant that Adam and Eve's physical bodies eventually died.

The Garden of Eden was destroyed before or during the flood of Noah's time; however, the Tree of Life wasn't destroyed. Rather, God moved it. The Tree of Life is in Paradise and eventually it will return to Earth (Revelation 2:7).

In the New Jerusalem, a river will flow from the throne of God, down the middle of a great street (Revelation 22:1-3). The Tree of Life is located on both sides of the river. This Revelation description seems to imply that the number of trees is more than one. Each month, the Tree will produce fruit.

In New Jerusalem, leaves on the Tree of Life will be for the healing of the nations (Revelation 22:2). In this instance, healing means the perpetual blessing of the new Heaven and Earth. Never again will Earth be plagued by physical or emotional pain.

Even though Adam and Eve eventually died because of their rebellion against God, they didn't forfeit God's love and care while they lived. God remained their father. God continued to interact with them and their offspring, including you and me in the 21st century. We have the opportunity to be in New Jerusalem.

We get instructions for living life in the 21st century from the Tree of Life's presence in the Garden of Eden and anticipated presence in New Jerusalem:

1) Despite our curiosity and desire to know everything—in this case, the species of the Tree of Life—we don't need to know everything. God promised that he has given us everything we need for a godly life (2 Peter 1:3).

2) We can't get back to the Tree of Life on our own merit. Figuratively, there are cherubim with big swords impeding our access. That's why God sent the Tree of Life to us in the form of his Son. Jesus came to Earth to give us the opportunity to enter Paradise and reconnect with the Tree that gives life.

3) When we accept Jesus as Savior, God comes to live in us, whether we physically inhabit a lush Eden or a sandy desert.

****

After Adam and Eve were expelled from Eden, humankind devolved morally. The Earth was filled with humankind who sinned. The sin grieved God. God determined to start over again. This time, God didn't create a new human type; rather, God used a family already on Earth. The man's name was Noah.

Noah was over 500 years old when God told him to build a giant water-proof vessel, an "ark". Technically, "ark" means a place of refuge. The vessel that Noah built was a refuge where Noah, his family, and certain animals and birds were saved from a flood that destroyed the known world.

Think about having a place of refuge. Where is yours in your home, at work, or at church? Mine used to be the local coffee shop. Now it's my blue chair.

Can you imagine how the neighbors ridiculed Noah? He was building a huge boat in the desert; yes, in the desert! Supposedly, it took Noah and his sons 100 years to build the vessel. Probably, individuals came from far and wide to see this oddity—a large ship in the desert. If Noah built it today in arid states like New Mexico or Arizona, the ark could be part of a summer vacation or a weekly trip to view updates.

Have you ever been ridiculed for doing something the Bible says to do? Examples are attending church services, refusing to have sex before marriage, or not cursing by using God's name.

30

When we are ridiculed, even when we know we are doing the right thing, we still feel deficient, embarrassed, and sometimes afraid.

What should we do when neighbors, co-workers, or even family members ridicule us? What should we do with our feelings? The answer is to take them to God, who helps us deal with our angst. Think about what King David did when he was on the run from King Saul. David poured out his heart to God multiple times. St. Paul told Christians who experienced trials to share their feelings with fellow believers. Telling God and friends can lessen the pain of ridicule.

Noah built his ark out of cypress wood which became a symbol of immortality to ancient peoples. They remembered that a cypress wood boat allowed individuals and animals to survive the flood. Today, in the Middle East, cypress trees are still planted in cemeteries to denote immortality. When you think of your life, what is your symbol of immortality? Mine is a cross.

Is Jesus your refuge in times of storms?

Twenty-first-century individuals didn't start righteously. All were born sinners and committed many sins during their lifetime. Remember that familiar Bible verse that tells us that God loved us so much that he sent his Son to die for us, even while we were lost in our sin (John 3:16)? By our choices in this earthly life, we decide where to spend our immortal life.

Receiving immortality from God by asking him to become our Savior doesn't absolve us from living righteously (sanctification). We have the ultimate "self-help" book for living a sanctified life. When I don't know what to do, I turn to the Bible for God's instructions. Where do you turn?

Delving Deeper

Chapter 1 is about characters in Genesis chapters 1 – 4. Who is the single most important character in this chapter. Why did you make this choice?

When do you think the Garden of Eden existed on planet Earth? For example, how many years ago? Or maybe you think it never existed on Earth.

Where did the Serpent come from who tempted Adam and Eve to eat from the Tree of Knowledge of Good and Evil? Who does the Serpent represent? Why a Serpent? Why not a camel, or an ox, or a spider? Read Job 1:6-12, Isaiah 14:1-5 and Ezekiel 28:1-5 to assist you in formulating your answers.

If Adam and Eve didn't disobey God and eat from the Tree of Knowledge of Good and Evil, would childbirth have been painless? Would there have even been childbirth? Did Eve give birth before she was expelled from Eden? Explain your answers.

Read Genesis 3:11-12: Why do you think that Adam blamed Eve for him eating from the Tree of Knowledge of Good and Evil? Why did Eve blame the Serpent? Who do you blame?

Chapter 2

A NEW DAY HAS COME

After Noah left the ark and he and his family began to repopulate Earth, a new day started. The lyrics of "A New Day Has Come"[3] tell of overcoming adversity and finding strength within us. The song speaks of triumph over challenges and the renewal of spirit. It invites listeners to leave behind the past and open their hearts to the limitless possibilities of a new day.

Chapter 2 portrays the earliest ancestors of the Judeo-Christian faith, heroes and heroines of a new day on Earth. The first ancestral couple was Abraham and his wife, Sarah, followed by their son, Isaac, and his wife, Rebecca. Abraham's grandson Jacob, two wives, and two concubines were the third set of ancestors. In Abraham's lineage, Joseph, his great-grandson, is the last of the great ancestors. The lives of these men and women are recorded in Genesis in the Bible. Their lives are composed of episodes that can instruct our lives in the 21st century.

Abraham was the first ancestor of the Jewish nation and of the Christian faith. The Bible tells us that Abraham was God's friend (Isaiah 41:8) and that Abraham's faith was counted as righteousness in God's sight (James 2:23). Although Abraham lived prior to God's Son coming to Earth, Abraham was "saved" through his faith in God's promise to reconcile the world to him through his Son.

At God's direction, Abraham and Sarah left their home in Haran. The God who talked to Abraham was new to Abraham. He wasn't one of the pantheon of Chaldean gods worshiped in Abraham and Sarah's culture. Abraham and Sarah traveled to Canaan, throughout Canaan, took a side trip to Egypt, and eventually settled at the great trees of Mamre near Hebron. The great trees at Mamre were most likely oak trees.

Oak trees symbolize strength and longevity in the sense of long life. Abraham and Sarah's decision to follow God showed strength. Few of us have the mental strength to leave the comfort of our home and travel to another country at a strange god's prompting. Some don't have sufficient physical strength to make this trip, likely by riding camels/donkeys from one location to another.

Have you ever done anything at God's prompting that requires strength? Your action need not be big. My girlfriend leaves for work in the morning 10 minutes early so she can drive around the block where another friend lives. While she circles the block, she prays for her friend's salvation. A simple act, yes, however, she has the endurance to do it day after day. She is committed to her friend's salvation over her own comfort and convenience.

God said, "The eyes of the Lord range throughout the earth to strengthen those whose hearts are fully committed to him" (2 Chronicles 16:9). God's roaming eyes saw Abraham and Sarah. God's eyes see each of us. God wants to see a fully committed person with the strength to do what he asks. Candidly, I know that I'm not 100% committed to God, i.e., over my comfort and convenience, but I want to be. Where are you on the comfort-commitment continuum?

An Israelite proverb is that the fear of the Lord adds length to life (Proverbs 10:27). God promises to be with his servants throughout life, even into their old age and gray hairs (Psalms 71:18). Abraham was 175 years old when he died. Sarah was 127 when she died. Likely, Sarah wasn't concerned about her hair turning gray. The two of them concentrated on following God.

Abraham and Sarah's story teaches us that Jesus-followers (Christians) don't have to worry about what they will do as they age. Importantly, we need not stagnate! Look at Abraham and Sarah! God called him to a new adventure when Abraham was in his seventh decade and Sarah in her sixth decade of life. Almost everything we read about this couple occurred after those ages.

God calls Christians to a different vision of life than the one painted by 21st-century culture.

Retirement isn't an option for followers of Jesus. Jesus doesn't call us to "retire" but to press on. A Christian shouldn't retire from growing into all Jesus calls him/her to be. At every age—in every decade of life—Jesus calls us to invest in eternity by investing in him and others.

Our work for Jesus should continue and grow until Jesus calls us home (John 15:7-8). Our impact for Jesus could increase in the final decades of life. During these decades, adults aren't distracted by child rearing or employment responsibilities.

It's political campaign season in the United States. Most of us receive requests to donate from a myriad of politicians. On each form, we are asked to indicate if we are retired. Retirement means we are no longer employed at a job from which we receive a salary. In reality, just because an individual is no longer employed at a salaried job doesn't mean he/she no longer works!

In my church, a new group started recently. The group is comprised of 50-year-plus individuals. The group is named Seasoned Christians. Seasoned means experienced, tested, weathered, even expert. Amusingly, "seasoned" also means flavored and spiced. I want to be defined by all of these words. Don't you? Instead of disengaging from life, Seasoned Christians maximize their spiritual impact in the church.

Seasoned Christians will have successes and failures. Their main aim/directive is to stay the course, to look for ways to work for God's glory throughout their life span.

Abraham and Sarah's story is one of successes and failures. Failures occurred when they lacked faith that God would do what God said he would do. Likely, your life mirrors theirs—successes and failures. Ideally, we learn from both.

Abraham's life leaves us with the question: "Is having a long life important?" Is a long life span more important than what you do with that life span?

Which is more important:
what you do with your life
or the length of your life?

****

Isaac was the second ancient ancestor of Jews and Christians. Isaac was the son whom God promised Abraham and Sarah. For the most part, Isaac's life was unremarkable. Isaac took no heroic actions and made no insightful comments. He wasn't defined as God's friend. Perhaps, Isaac's actions or lack of actions is the reason he's an Israelite patriarch. Not every Christian or church member is a standout. In *Paradise Lost*, John Milton[4] wrote "They also serve who only stand and wait."

When Isaac was about 16 years old, God commanded Abraham to take him to Mount Moriah (Genesis 22:1-19). There, God told Abraham to sacrifice Isaac to God. Think about the agonizing wait that Abraham and Sarah had before the birth of Isaac. Now, God tells Abraham to offer his son as a burnt offering, in essence, to kill Isaac.

Abraham didn't hesitate or question God's command. He focused on obeying God. Early the morning after Abraham received God's instruction, Abraham, Isaac, and two servants started walking toward Mount Moriah. Noteworthy, there's no biblical record that Abraham told Sarah about God's command. Nor did Sarah accompany Abraham and Isaac to Mount Moriah.

During the trek, Abraham didn't become ensnared in Satan's lies or become confused by his limited understanding of God's instructions to him. Imagine the confusing thoughts that Satan brought to Abraham's mind during the three-day journey to Mount Moriah, i.e., "Surely God doesn't mean for you to sacrifice Isaac? A God that really loved and cared about you would never require you to kill your beloved son." Likely, Abraham agonized over the pain that a dead Isaac would cause his much-loved Sarah. These thoughts were made worse when Isaac innocently asked his father, "Where is the lamb for the burnt offering?" (Genesis 22:7).

Most of us were in situations when our minds became entangled in a problem. We worried about the problem as a dog gnaws at a bone. Our thoughts went around and around as we tried to formulate every possible solution, that is, a human-identified solution. Can you imagine an alternative way to behave than getting mired down in these types of thoughts?

Abraham's actions are instructive when we find ourselves in a shaky situation. For Abraham, the solution was simple—obey God—even when Abraham didn't understand how following God would work out for his good. Abraham obeyed God, believing that God would keep his promise to give him and Sarah an heir.

When Abraham and Isaac reached Mount Moriah, Abraham built an altar, arranged wood on it, and tied Isaac on top of the altar. Isaac was aware of Abraham's intent. Abraham's actions showed clearly that his father was going to sacrifice him on the altar.

Likely, Satan whispered slyly to Isaac: "You're a big, strong boy. Don't let your father tie you to the altar. You know what he is going to do—you're going to be killed! Escape! Save yourself! Nothing good is going to come of this situation." Importantly, Isaac didn't listen to Satan; he made no effort to escape.

When Abraham raised his knife, prepared to slay Isaac, an angel told Abraham not to kill Isaac. The angel commended Abraham for trusting God enough to be willing to sacrifice his son. Abraham looked up and saw a ram caught by the horns in a nearby thicket. Abraham killed the ram and offered it to God as a burnt offering.

What do your children learn when they see you obeying God when it is inconvenient, even hurts? What message do you give your children when your only answer to their, "Why" is: "Because the Bible says so."

Identify a time in your life when you obeyed God when it wasn't logical!

The Hebrew word for thicket comes from the word *çâba,*[5] which means to entwine in the sense of inter-woven branches. In English, entanglement means to twist together and to ensnare. Entanglements confuse us when they occur in our lives. Examples of entanglement are being in a codependent relationship, working in competitive or antagonistic workplaces, living among family conflicts, having struggles at school, or struggles, and clashes with neighbors.

What should we do when (not if) entanglements occur in our lives? Some individuals simply back down or back away from them. They give in, give up, or give out, i.e., leave the situation. Others seek a support group or some type of mental health therapy. A newly touted approach to dealing with entanglements is exercise. All are useful to some extent; however, they are coping mechanisms, not methods to solve the original problem.

When experienced hikers encounter a thicket, they rarely try to go through it. Instead, they navigate around it. Christians have a better, more efficient and effective way to deal with entanglements than hikers. That way is navigating toward God and his instruction book, the Bible. Below are a few Bible verses that can reframe our thinking on entanglements.

> Anxiety in a man's heart weighs him down (Proverbs 12:17). Don't be anxious about anything, instead tell God (Philippians 6:6). Which of you by being anxious can add a single hour to his span of life? (Matthew 6:27).

Let not your hearts be troubled, neither let them be afraid (John 14:27). Cast your burden on the Lord, and he will sustain you (Psalm 55:22). If God is for us, who can be against us (Romans 8:31)? For those who love God, all things work together for good (Romans 8:28).

In the future what are you going to do when you encounter entanglements? Recycle your thoughts, turn to therapy, hit the gym and exercise, or turn to God and his instruction book?

****

When Isaac was about 40 years of age, he married Rebecca. Isaac loved Rebecca (Genesis 24:67). Rebecca gave birth to twin boys. Esau was the firstborn. Jacob was second born. As the firstborn son, Esau was the heir to Isaac's wealth. Jacob was jealous of Esau's birthright. He wanted the birthright (right of the firstborn son) because of the wealth and prestige that went with the position.

The Bible recorded that one day Esau returned to camp after a time away, probably hunting. Esau saw Jacob cooking red lentil stew. Esau was hungry to the point of being famished. Esau asked Jacob for some stew. Jacob said that he would give Esau the lentil stew but only if Esau swore to give Jacob his birthright. Esau swore the oath in exchange for lentil stew.

Think of the difference in value of some lentil stew versus being the heir to Isaac's wealth. From this episode, we learn not to exchange being a ransomed child of God destined for Heaven for temporary wealth and fame on Earth. Did you get any additional instructions from this episode?

In Bible times, a father gave his blessing to his heir. Isaac planned to give his blessing to Esau. Conveying the blessing was an important ritual. Rebecca crafted a detailed (Genesis 27:5-17) plot for Jacob to dress like Esau, enter a blind Isaac's tent, and receive Isaac's hereditary blessing.

Rebecca schemed to circumvent her own cultural values and Isaac's wish that Esau be his heir. I believe her reason was love. Although Isaac loved Rebecca, the only person Rebecca is recorded as loving was Jacob (Genesis 25:28).

When, if ever, did Jesus by words or actions advocate scheming behaviours?

Jesus' behaviour to his human brothers and sisters is diametrically opposite to Jacob and Rebecca's conniving behaviour. Jesus invites each of us to come to him and live with him. We don't have to barter for Jesus' gift of salvation. Freely, Jesus nourishes us with himself and his words, i.e., "the one who feeds on me will live because of me" (John 6:57). There is a myriad of motives for our actions on a continuum of selfishness to complete altruism. It's difficult to compare Jesus' selfless love to us with our personal motives and schemes.

****

Over subsequent years, Isaac and Rebecca's home life deteriorated. Esau's anger grew because of Jacob's successful ruse to obtain Isaac's legacy. Esau was determined to kill Jacob as soon as Isaac died. Again, Rebecca intervened. She had Isaac send Jacob to her brother, Laban, in Paddan Aram for the ostensible reason of finding a non-Canaanite wife. The real reason was to get Jacob away from Esau.

After arriving in Paddan Aram, Jacob met his cousin, Rachel, and loved her. Jacob worked for seven years to receive Rachel as a wife. On his wedding night, Rachel's father (Laban) schemed for Jacob to marry and sleep with Rachel's sister, Leah, rather than Rachel. Jacob worked an additional seven years to obtain Rachel as his wife. The Bible paints a picture of both Jacob and Laban as schemers.

After almost two decades living in Paddan Aram, Jacob decided to return to Canaan with his family. Jacob wanted to return as a successful man who had the wealth to care for his large family. By this time, Jacob had two wives, two concubines, 11 sons, and one daughter. Jacob used superstitious actions to attempt to increase his flock size and thus his wealth (Genesis 30:37-43). Jacob's superstitious behavior showed belief in a power other than God.

Before we are too critical of Jacob's superstitious behavior, let's look at our own behavior. Some Americans read their horoscope daily to plan their day. Horoscopes depend on the alignment of planets and stars in the sky. Bible principles can and should direct our actions in any

day, hour, and minute. Further, Christians have the
Holy Spirit to instruct and guide them.

What was the last superstitious action you used, i.e., knock on wood?

On the return trip from Paddan Aram to
Canaan, Laban waylaid Jacob. Laban accused Jacob
of stealing his household gods (images). Jacob didn't
steal them. Unbeknownst to Jacob, Rachel took
them.

When Laban searched Jacob's camp, Rachel
sat on a camel saddle. Jacob's household images
were under it. Rachel told her father that she couldn't
rise from the saddle because she had her menstrual
flow (Genesis 31:35). Thus, Rachel schemed to
circumvent Laban's aim to locate images of his gods.

Despite Jacob's superstitious and scheming
behaviour, God saw value in him. God changed
Jacob's name to Israel. Synonyms for Jacob's
offspring were Children of Israel and Israelites.
Jacob's favourite wife, Rachel is considered the
mother of Judaism. Jacob and Rachel's lives show
21st-century Christians that we don't have to be
perfect to be useful to God. We only need Jesus'
forgiveness.

****

Joseph was the oldest son of Jacob and
Rachel and the eleventh-born son of Jacob. Joseph
was the fourth ancient ancestor of Jews and
Christians. Despite Joseph's birth order, Jacob
named Joseph "heir" because Joseph was Rachel's

firstborn son. Jacob treated Joseph better than he treated his other sons. Joseph's life is recorded in Genesis chapters 37-46.

Jacob's preferential (favoritism) treatment of Joseph and Joseph's clueless behavior in telling his brothers his dreams, where they bowed to him, caused the brothers to be jealous of Joseph. When Joseph was about 17 years of age, his brothers sold Joseph to Ishmaelite traders. From age 17-30, Joseph was enslaved or imprisoned in a foreign country, Egypt.

Here is the backstory of Joseph getting to Egypt: Except for Benjamin, Jacob's sons were Joseph's half-brothers. Yet, these brothers sold Joseph into slavery for 20 pieces of silver. Joseph's brothers knew the degradation that occurred in a slave's life. Joseph would be abused on both the trek to Egypt and as a slave in Egypt. The brothers didn't care. Similarly, they didn't care that their father, Jacob, would be devastated over the loss of Joseph.

Likely, 6-9 brothers were involved. When the selling price was divided among them, each received 2-3 silver pieces. The brothers sold Joseph not to get rich, but to get rid of him.

When Joseph was about 30 years of age, Pharaoh had a dream. Joseph was called to interpret it. After interpreting the dream for Pharaoh, Pharaoh freed Joseph from prison. Pharaoh made Joseph second only to himself in power in Egypt. Pharaoh gave Joseph a wife. She was Aseneth, a daughter of the chief priest of On (Genesis 41:45). Joseph and Aseneth had two sons, Manasseh and Ephraim. Joseph lived the remainder of his life in Egypt.

The Bible recorded information on Sarah, Rebecca, Leah/Rachel. Why not on Aseneth?

Despite this seeming happy ending, it's a story of heartache. Favoritism started it all. In this episode, Jacob favored Joseph over his other sons. Favoritism is a preference or partiality for certain people or groups based on our personal biases. Personal biases often focus on race, skin color, gender, socioeconomic status, religion, method of dress, and accent.

Two other biases are anchoring bias and confirmation bias. Anchoring bias means we keep the same attitude toward another as formed with the first contact. Confirmation bias is believing that an individual or group is deserving of favor. Currently, in the United States, we see much confirmation and anchoring bias. Whatever the source of favoritism, it leads to prejudice and discrimination against non-preferred individuals.

Favoritism is the opposite of God's command to love all individuals equally. Favoritism causes the devaluation of people for whom Jesus died. Favoritism demonstrates an ignorance of God's values. The Bible is clear: God doesn't show favoritism. Neither should we, his human creatures! Often, Christians believe favoritism is okay, citing that the Israelites were favored over other ancient nations, tribes. In reality, God selected the Israelites as his chosen people (not his favorite people). And

God chose the Israelites for God's glory, not their glory (Isaiah 49:3).

Jesus-believers are called to reject favoritism in all forms. Christians are to treat individuals equally, showing love and respect to all. Read the following verses from both the Old and New Testaments, which contain God's views on favoritism:

- Do not pervert justice; do not show partiality to the poor or favoritism to the great, but judge your neighbor fairly (Leviticus 19:15).
- God shows no partiality and accepts no bribes (Deuteronomy 10:17).
- God....accepts from every nation the one who fears him and does what is right (Acts 10:24-24).
- God doesn't show favoritism (Romans 2:11). There are no favorites before God (Colossians 3:25).
- Believers in our glorious Lord Jesus Christ must not show favoritism (James 2:1).
- Do nothing out of favoritism (1 Timothy 5:21).

Frequently, favoritism operates on a subconscious level. Favoritism is ingrained in American culture/society. Only rarely are individuals able to eliminate favoritism from their behavior; however, they can be aware that favoritism operates subconsciously in most of us. Leon Festinger[6] proposed that eventually we think like we are required to act. For example, because we are required by law to treat racial minorities equally with Whites, we eventually treat them equally.

There are two other sides to favoritism: One—at times we are the favorite. When we are favored, it's easy to slide into a sense of entitlement. Sometimes we believe that we are more deserving than others. Eventually, we may attempt to slide by with substandard efforts because we are favored. Usually, this type of favoritism doesn't last long, particularly in the workplace.

Two—sometimes we see another person being favored. No matter what we do, it isn't enough to be treated as positively as this other person is treated. It's hard not to feel resentful and jealous, whether in a family or in the workplace. Conflicts result because we are envious of the preferred person.

From time to time, favoritism occurs in a church. Greg Paul[7] identified categories of favoritism seen in the local church. They include favoring the rich over the poor, similar over different, insider versus outsider, male versus female, and social circumstances.

The question is whether or not we should make the actor (perpetrator), particularly if the person is a pastor, aware that she/he is showing favoritism. That is a tough call. If favoritism is harming the health of the church/organization or the reputation of the church/organization, the answer is "Yes."

Then, the question is, "How do I go about having this conversation with my pastor or boss?" I'm going to deal with initiating a conversation with a pastor; however, you can apply it to a workplace setting, even a family setting. Begin by pray that

God's will, not yours, will be done in the conversation. This conversation isn't about you.

Then, determine not to be confrontational or argumentative. Think about how you can have a collegial conversation. Determine to be humble. Know that this discussion may require more than one meeting to resolve the problem. Keep trying to make the point. You believe it's accurate. Also, don't get sidetracked from your main purpose.

Remember, you've been thinking and praying about the situation for weeks, maybe months. In contrast, this meeting may be the first time the pastor hears that she/he is showing favoritism. The pastor's first reaction will likely be defensiveness and disagreement. Just as you needed time to ponder and pray about the situation, so will the pastor. Set up a follow-up meeting.

Don't gossip about your pending conversation. True, the Bible instructs us to share our burdens with fellow Jesus-believers. You can solicit needed situational prayers without giving specifics. Saying something as innocuous as, "I am going to have a meeting with the pastor and need your prayers," is saying too much. This statement can generate gossip in the church. It's okay and biblical to solicit prayers; however, ask fellow-believers to pray for an unnamed prayer request.

Finally, prepare for the meeting! Organize your thoughts and points you want to make. You may even want to keep a record of where you believe favoritism occurred in the church. Naming specific situations (maybe even dates) adds strength to your assertion.

If this strategy doesn't resolve the problem of pastoral favoritism, what then? The "then" is to do what the Bible tells you to do:

> "If your brother or sister sins, go and point out their fault, just between the two of you. But if they will not listen, take one or two others along, so that 'every matter may be established by the testimony of two or three witnesses.' (Matthew 18:15-17).

What happens next is ordained by God. You have done your part.

Delving Deeper

Before the Flood, Noah was described as a righteous man. Was he a righteous man in his life after the Flood? What does being righteous in God's sight mean? Sinless? Perfect? Forgiven? Are you righteous in God's sight?

Discuss what could have occurred if Abraham and Sarah refused God's direction to go and live in Canaan. What would have been the impact on the Jewish religion, birth of the Messiah, the New Testament church?

Why is Isaac's story in the Bible? Would the record of ancient Israelite fathers have been just as effective without the Isaac episodes? Why or why not?

How can schemers such as Jacob, Rachel, and Rebecca be considered great Israelite ancestors?

In the Bible, we aren't told if Joseph repented of his clueless behavior of broadcasting his dreams to his brother or if Jacob repented of his favoritism of Joseph. What do you think—repentance or non-repentance?

Chapter 3

Knockin on Heaven's Door

Chapter 3 is titled "Knockin on Heaven's Door." Written and sung by Bob Dylan[8] as a movie soundtrack, "Knockin on Heaven's Door" touches our souls as we attempt to access God.

Perhaps the best-known verse in the song is:

I can hear that thunder roar
Echoing down from god's distance shore
I can hear him calling for my soul
I feel like I'm knockin' on heaven's door.[8]

Most of Chapter 3 focuses on building the Tabernacle, the way ancient Israelites knocked on God's door. Moses was the Israelite leader when the Israelite/Jewish religion began on the Sinai Peninsula. Many components present in Christianity and in Christian churches today were initiated when the Tabernacle was built with its candles, incense, bread, etc.

All Tabernacle structures and furniture built on the Sinai Peninsula were replicas of heavenly structures. Each was planned carefully by God to represent a heavenly truth. Their purpose and craftsmanship apply to our lives in the 21st century. Chapter three identifies these linkages and describes their significance to 21st-century Christian life.

****

Christians know the sweet story of baby Moses being saved from sure death by his mother, Jochebed. She built a floating bulrush basket and placed him in the Nile River. We know the romantic story of Moses helping Jethro's daughters draw water for their flocks. Later, Moses married one of the daughters. We've read of Moses' encounter with God, who appeared in a burning bush. We rejoice with Moses when he parted the Red Sea and the Israelites passed through the Sea on dry ground (Exodus 14:15-31). We know Moses spoke for God when the Tabernacle was built.

Rarely is the story of Moses, the murderer, told in a children's Sunday school lesson or in a church sermon. Here is the story: Moses saw an Egyptian beating an Israelite (Exodus 2:11-15). Looking both ways, Moses saw no one watching him. Moses killed the Egyptian and buried the body in the sand. Moses knew his murderous action was wrong. When confronted about it, Moses fled Egypt to Midian, outside of Pharaoh's control.

Moses' murder of an Egyptian was an impulsive act. Impulsive acts occur quickly; often, they are spontaneous. Little up-front thought goes into the action. Moses didn't ponder the effect of murdering an Egyptian before doing it. Before Moses hid the Egyptian's body, was possibly the first time he thought through his action, including its impact on his life as a noble in Pharaoh's court.

Often, our actions are good; ones Christians should do. Moses stopping one man from beating another was an admirable action. What wasn't admirable was how Moses stopped the beating. He murdered the perpetrator.

Is murdering someone ever okay?

Most of us aren't murderers in that we don't take the physical life of a person. On the other hand, sometimes we take the reputation and thereby the livelihood of a person. The two avenues we use are slander and gossip. The outcome of slander is long-lived. Once lies are told about a person, it's difficult to remove them. Gossip destroys a person's reputation in the community and in the workplace.

So the question is, how does a Christian deal with slander (murder) of their name? One way is to pray for the slanderer and about the slanderous remark. With prayer, God can remove the slander or the sting of it. Frequently, when we are slandered, our attempts to clear our reputation fail. At times, attempting to undercut a slanderous remark calls attention to it and spreads it further.

Some other ways of dealing with slander come from the Bible. Saint Peter wrote, "Do not repay evil with evil or insult with insult but with blessing (1 Peter 3:9). You are seen as taking the high road when you repay a slanderous remark with a kind word. Succinctly put, you won't be overcome by evil but will overcome evil with good (Romans 12:21).

Christians aren't immune to slandering and gossiping about others, even other Christians. God, the perfect judge, doesn't look positively on our use of slander. Here are some Bible references about slander.

- On Judgment Day, individuals will give account for every careless word they have spoken (Matthew 12:36-37). By our words, we will be acquitted and condemned. Wouldn't you prefer acquittal? Don't these verse cause you to shake?
- If we guard our lips, we preserve our lives, but individuals who speak rashly will come to ruin (Proverbs 13:3). That verse is a statement—there is no wiggle room on what will happen if we speak rashly.
- A fool's mouth is his undoing; his lips are a snare to his soul (Proverbs 18:7-8). A gossip's words are like choice morsels; they go into a person's innermost parts.
- Rid yourself of all malice, deceit, hypocrisy, envy, and slander of every kind (1 Peter 2:1).

****

The Israelite Tabernacle builders needed wood. On the Sinai Peninsula, the most common source of wood was the acacia (*shittah*[5]) tree. Acacia wood is beautiful, light, and practically indestructible. It was ideal for the multiple moves the Israelites made in their 40-year journey on the Sinai Peninsula and final march into Canaan.

In the Tabernacle, indestructible acacia wood anticipated Jesus, the Christ. Isaiah (53:2) described the Messiah as "a root out of dry ground," similar to the acacia tree growing out of desert soil. Although acacia wood is only virtually indestructible, Jesus is fully indestructible. The indestructible Jesus came back to life after being crucified and dead. Burnt offerings are no longer needed for sins to be forgiven and individuals reconciled to God. With his death and resurrection, Jesus completed the reconciliation process once for all.

Most of us would love our epitaph to read "_____ (your name) was indestructible in his/her walk with Jesus." In reality, there was only one indestructible person who walked or will walk the Earth. That person was Jesus, the Son of God. How indestructible we are depends on how close we stay to Jesus.

Reread the epitaph in the previous paragraph. How can you start to make that epitaph true for you? Each of us can and should explore ways for us that remain consistent with God's statutes. What works for one person won't necessarily work for another. We need to investigate various methods, rejecting some, accepting some. As we mature in our Christian faith, our walk with God changes, and our methods to stay close to Jesus change.

For the past decade, I've been a member of a group of women who have the purpose of daily prayer, study of God's Word, service to others, and evangelism. Having these identified daily purposes gives structure to my Christian walk. Even though I don't participate in the same activities daily, i.e., say the Lord's Prayer, I pray daily. No, the activities don't make me indestructible, but they make me more committed as I live a life for Jesus in the 21st century.

The downside of building with acacia wood was the two gray straight thorns (as much as eight inches long) that grew at the base of each tree leaf. What are we to learn from God requiring the Israelites to build from (work with) a plant that could hurt them?

A possible answer is that although God gave a new religion to his people on the Sinai peninsula, the consequences of Adam and Eve's sin remained. Humankind still lived with thorns and pain even when following God's instructions painstakingly. Our work can wound us even when that work is given by God and done for God. Recall Mother Theresa's ministry.

The Hebrew word for thorn is *shayith*[5,] which translates as "trash." Trash is debris (often from plants) worth little or nothing. Generally, trash is thrown away or burned.

Trash is a symbol for individuals who reject Jesus as Savior.

Was the religion God gave Moses on Mount Sinai trash? No, but eventually it was set aside. Replaced by the indestructible doctrine of redemption through Jesus Christ, salvation for humankind through the atoning death of God's Son. Remember, Martin Luther's mantra: "Christ alone, grace alone, faith alone." The Tabernacle on Mount Sinai was a stopgap measure until Jesus, the Christ, came and brought salvation through grace alone.

****

Linen was the only cloth used in the Tabernacle. Tabernacle linen came from flax plants. The Hebrew word for Tabernacle linen is *shêsh*[5] and means "fine linen." *Shêsh*[5] denoted Egyptian linen of peculiar whiteness and excellence. Fine linen was soft and flexible, yet strong. It had a luster, or sheen, which made it look like silk.

In ancient Egypt, fine linen was a mark of quality and associated with wealth and rank. As slaves in Egypt, the Israelites didn't have much, if any, fine linen; however, when they left Egypt, the Egyptians gave them tribute. The tribute included fine linen clothes and cloth.

In Revelation, St. John used "clean, shining linen" as a symbol for purity. Purity means spotless, stainless, and free from pollutants, including moral fault or guilt. Purity is a quality that all 21st-century Christians should strive for. Purity means we are free from guilt in the way we think about, speak about, and act toward others.

We want to keep our hearts pure (like s*hêsh*[5]), but at times, our life is filled with irrelevant thoughts and actions. Do you attempt to keep your thoughts pure? If wrong thoughts enter your mind, don't ruminate on them. Instead, call the Holy Spirit to remove them from you. The good news is that the Holy Spirit wants to make and keep you pure.

When did you last agree with God about your sins?

Linen curtains separated the Tabernacle from the remainder of the Israelite camp. The area inside the curtains was seen as holy, as pure. Also, curtains composed some walls of the Tent of Meeting, that is, the space which contained the Ark of the Covenant in the Most Holy of Holies and the worship furniture in the Holy of Holies.

The Jerusalem Temple in Jesus' lifetime had a linen curtain that separated the Most Holy of Holies from the Holy of Holies. This curtain was named Veil. The Temple Veil mirrored the curtain in the Tent of Meeting that was fabricated on the Sinai Peninsula.

When Jesus died, the Jerusalem Temple curtain or Veil tore from top to bottom. God made the tear. Jesus' death opened a way for believers in Jesus as Savior to have direct access to God. Christians are no longer separated from God. No curtain obscures God from his children and his children from God. We can experience Jesus' purity.

After we are saved, our view of God can be veiled, diminished, because of our sin. We don't need to be "resaved," but we do need to pursue continued contact with God to remain pure.

Keeping an optimal relationship with God is intentional and ongoing work. We don't always remain pure in thoughts, words, and actions. God made a way for us to be reconciled to him and his purity. Having a pure, clean heart is as simple as going to God, agreeing with God about our sins, and asking God to forgive them. If you haven't read 1 John 1:9, now would be a great time. Be sure to follow its instructions.

One of Saint Paul's explicit points on separation between believers and non-believers is summarized in the statement, "Therefore come out from among them and be separate" (2 Corinthians 6:17). Does this mean that Christians should live in a community, possibly even a cult-like community, so they can be separate from the world and pure? No!

Once saved we are new beings, therefore separate from the world. The Holy Spirit lives in us. True, we come into contact with many non-Christian individuals in our community and work lives. Although we interact with them and at times socialize with them, these individuals shouldn't be best friends forever (BFF). Our BFFs should be believers who have Jesus as the most important part of their lives.

Many of us, particularly new Christians, ponder what to do if our BFF isn't a Christian. Should we drop the friendship, continue the same types of conversations with the BFF as before salvation, go to the same places, and do the same things after salvation as before salvation? We worry that if we change our behavior too fast and too much, we will be accused of acting holier-than-thou. Some biblical suggestions are:

1) Pray. Ask God how to be a witness to your BFF.

2) Witness. Witness to your BFF, about the goodness, including salvation, of Jesus. Be sure to share your testimony, including what Jesus is doing in your life. Importantly, don't use a "holier than thou" tone of voice when you share (witness).

3) Separate. Separate yourself from the activities that the two of you previously did together, which you know aren't God-pleasing. Discuss them with your friend. Explain why you are changing your behavior.

4) Reorder. As your circle of friends fills with Spirit-filled individuals who think and feel like you do, you will most likely decrease the time with your former BFFs. You may grieve ending a relationship. Turn your grief over to God; talk it out with him.

****

At God's direction, the Israelites made a candlestick from gold for the Tent of Meeting. The candlestick had seven stems that included the middle stem. Olive oil lamps were set on the end of each stem. If you are familiar with the Israelite menorah, that was the lampstand's shape.

Each Lampstand branch was decorated with almond buds. Almond buds symbolized God's watchful presence over the Israelites. In the Hebrew language, the name for the almond tree is s*hâqêd*[5] from a word meaning to be watchful, alert, on the lookout, and sleepless. God said that he is watching to see that his word is fulfilled on Earth (Jeremiah 1:12). Job named God a "watcher of men" (Job 7:20).

If you knew that someone was watching you, how would your behavior, your actions, change? Someone is watching you!!! The watcher isn't some famous person, a parent, politician, or pastor. The watcher is the holy God. God isn't watching you to catch you doing something wrong or something salacious. God watches you to help you do good.

By using the almond tree symbol in the Tabernacle, God provided both reassurance and caution to the Israelites. Reassurance that God was always watching over them. Caution so his children would remain alert to situations that could detract from keeping God the primary focus of their lives.

Are you watching God?
God's watching you.

Paul instructed Timothy to "Watch your life and doctrine closely" (1 Timothy 4:16). If the godly Timothy had to watch his life and doctrine, most assuredly Jesus-followers in the 21st century need to watch theirs.

At one point in my career, I taught online (computer-based) courses to university students. In those courses, faculty and students rarely meet. Students were in Africa as missionaries, in Guam as sailors, or elsewhere across the globe. Faculty watched as students implemented course content and completed assignments. By university policy, the faculty member had 24 hours to respond to a student's questions.

Faculty-student interactions in an online course reflect how God works with us. Constantly, God monitors our behavior. When we get off track, God sends us messages to readjust our thinking and behavior. Unlike my interaction with students, God doesn't take up to 24 hours to respond. Nor does God use email and electronics.

Just as a student must open and read faculty-sent emails for course success, Jesus-followers must read messages from God. The best place to get those messages is from the Bible.

Because God watches over us, doesn't mean that we can float along in our relationship with him. We must stay alert and on track with God's guidelines for a successful Christian life. Jesus warned Peter, "Watch and pray that you may not fall into temptation. The spirit indeed is willing, but the flesh is weak" (Matthew 26:40).

Are you watching and praying so you don't fall into temptation? In what areas of your life are you neglecting to watch that you are following God's instructions? Below are some ways that we can watch our lives throughout the day:

- Put away our phone or tablet for an hour. Think about God in place of scrolling through news, messages, and social media.
- Stash devotionals in readily accessible places. Grab and read from them throughout the day.

- Place a Bible verse in a visible area. Mine is on the bathroom mirror.
- As you drive your car, listen to Christian music or a podcast. Listen to a section from an audio Bible.
- Set a midday alarm. Pray and meditate for five minutes when the alarm goes off.

****

The only source of light in the Tent of Meeting was the seven oil lamps on the golden candlestick stems. The lamps illuminated the area around them. The question is: Do we illuminate the area around us, i.e., in our home, at our workplace, at community events to include in our church?

Repeatedly, Old Testament writers told the Israelites that God was their light. In turn, they were to reflect God's light to the surrounding nations. Jesus continued this same theme in the New Testament. He told believers: "You are the light of the world...let your light shine before others, that they may see your good works and give glory to your Father in heaven" (Matthew 5:14-16). Notice our good deeds aren't for our personal or tribal glory but for God's glory.

In the 21st century, God gives his people (Christians) the same message he gave the Israelites 4000 years ago, i.e., reflect (shine) God's light. As a Jesus-reflector, we are to shine our light on individuals of all races, nations, religions, and preferences. Take about five minutes and enumerate how you are shining our light and ways you need to level up your reflection of Jesus.

Remember the song you learned as a child? It went something like this:

This little light of mine, I'm gonna let it shine.
This little light of mine, I'm gonna let it shine.
This little light of mine, I'm gonna let it shine.
Let it shine, Let it shine, Let it shine.

When I read about the golden candlestick and olive oil lamps, my mind goes to words of William Shakespeare[9] in *The Merchant of Venice,* "How far that little candle throws his beams! So shines a good deed in a weary world." Your small kindnesses, my small kindnesses, are rays of light in a dark world. For us, the dark Tent of Meeting is the society we live in. How can we shine our light over a great distance?

I ask myself, how far my light shines.
My answer disappointed me.

Most of us are satisfied to shine our light a short distance. We don't aspire to be a radiant star seen from millions of miles away. Yet, God can take the light of our tiny candle and use it for his good and glory, even to the other side of the globe. We don't have to be Billy Graham, Max Lucado, or Priscilla Shriver. We can just be us, a woman or a man who follows Jesus.

When you reflect Jesus' light—when you follow Jesus—individuals around you notice. Often, others say that there is something different about my husband (Bruce). He doesn't curse, isn't a drunkard, is faithful to me, and polite. My girlfriends say they "just love him." My husband is the finest Christian man I know. Do individuals say that about you? How can you change your behavior so that individuals do? Remember your desired epitaph?

Most of us show distortion when we reflect Jesus. As sinful humankind, even after we are saved, we remain flawed reflections of Jesus. That doesn't mean we should stop trying to emit the light of Jesus.

A possible reason for our flawed reflection of Jesus is our lack of awareness. Awareness (mindfulness, alertness, discernment) is a behavior that most individuals in the 21st century lack. We don't spend time thinking about how to be aware of Jesus so we can better reflect him. Equally true, we are unaware of how much our own behavior negatively affects our witness for Jesus.

Jesus said that individuals around us should see our good works and glorify God. What good works are neighbors, friends, and acquaintances seeing in you? A really simple answer of what they should see in you is the fruit of the Holy Spirit, i.e., love, joy, peace, patience, kindness, goodness (Galatians 5:22-23). Radiating the fruit of the Spirit isn't to make us well-liked, receive work promotions, get elected to a prominent position, or negotiate special privileges for our children.

****

In the Tabernacle, the Presence Bread (loaf of bread) symbolized each of the 12 Israelite tribes' presence before God. The loaves were placed on a table in the Tent of Meeting. The bread was consecrated (set aside, made holy, blessed) by priests. Often named the "bread of the Presence," a more accurate Hebrew translation is "bread of the face."

The Presence Bread pointed to the Children of Israel's lives with God. As the Presence Bread stood before God in the Tent of Meeting, in the 21st century, Christians stand before Jesus. We live an alive life because Jesus lives in us. Remember, Jesus said:

> I am the living bread that came down from heaven. Whoever eats this bread will live forever. This bread is my flesh, which will be given for the life of the world (John 6:51).

The Presence Bread was made from finely ground wheat flour, olive oil, and salt. Ancient peoples named wheat the "giving grain" and associated it with the cycle of life and death. For Israelites, wheat symbolized life from God and with God. Notice the bread was unleavened; it contained no yeast. Neither loaves of bread nor Israelites were to be puffed up.

Most likely, the Israelites didn't have a millstone to grind wheat kernels on the Sinai Peninsula. Instead, a mortar and pestle were used to crush wheat kernels into flour. Then, the ground wheat was finely sifted to free it from coarseness, unevenness, and empty husks.

Jesus passed through the grindstones while on Earth. He suffered trials and temptations. Like fine wheat flour in the Presence Bread, Jesus showed no trace of unevenness or coarseness. We shouldn't be surprised when we, like wheat kernels, are ground and sifted by God to make us a purer consistency.

In the 21st century, Americans don't pray to be finely ground flour. We dislike temptation and trials that refine us. Often, we fail both. We prefer a calm, serene, smooth life with minimal turmoil.

Each Sabbath, new loaves were placed on the Table of the Presence Bread. The older loaves were removed and eaten by priests. The offeror/receiver obtained no special merit from the exchange of old and new bread loaves at the door of the Tent of Meeting.

In the 21st century, Christians give offerings—time, talent, and treasury—to God. Our loaf of Presence Bread goes to pay ministers' salaries, church mortgage or maintenance, and support church programs, etc. We receive no special merit from our gifts.

Do you anticipate receiving an "attaboy/attagirl" in Heaven for what you did on Earth?

Recently, I read that our gifts to para-church organizations, i.e., Samaritan's Purse, Focus on the Family, can't take the place of money to the church. For instance, we can't say, "Instead of giving my money to the church this week, I'm giving it to Samaritan's Purse." From this perspective, gifts to para-church organizations are in addition to offerings to the church. What do you think? Can you substitute gifts to para-church organizations for gifts to the local church?

Our gifts (time, talent, tithe) to God memorialize all God gives to us by giving God a small return gift. When Christians give to God, they do so knowing that all they have is from God. We can't give anything to God that God doesn't already have in abundance and that God didn't first give us. We give to God out of the abundance of our love for him and his gifts to us.

As loaves of Presence Bread, we too exist before God. Full awareness, full realization, that we live in God's presence, is intimidating. Living in God's presence means we set aside time for prayer, Bible reading, church attendance, etc.

When God told the Israelites to replace Presence Bread loaves each Sabbath, he gave the Israelites a schedule for making offerings. This schedule given on the Sinai Peninsula provides instruction for our lives in the 21st century. We should have a schedule for presenting gifts to him. Sunday is a great time to do that but not the only time.

Delving Deeper

Do you murder individuals in your environment, i.e., home, church, workplace, community? How can you stop murdering them?

How do you evaluate and level up your Christian walk? Is this method sufficient, or do you need to make some adjustments given that God is always watching you? Name 3-5 adjustments you want to make.

What is the curtain that protects you from the world? How could you strengthen the curtain?

On the Sinai Peninsula, the oil lamps on the golden candlestick were to be trimmed so that they burned through the night. After the Israelites entered the Promised Land, the lamps didn't burn throughout the night (1 Samuel 3:1-2). The lamps went out! How could the rarity of visions among the Israelites at this time be related to oil lamps not burning throughout the night?

How are you, like the loaves of Presence Bread, always before God? How can attending church services be an advantage as you live your 21st-century life?

Chapter 4

IN THE PROMISED LAND

Chuck Berry wrote the lyrics to the song "Promised Land" in 1965 at the height of the civil rights movement.[10] "Promised Land" deals with a mythical place where freedom and equality are assured, much like the Children of Israel's view of the land promised to them by God.

Biblical stories about Israelites entering Perea (east side of the Jordan River) and Canaan and adjusting to life there are told in Joshua, Judges, and Ruth. This land was collectively known as the Promised Land because God promised it to the Israelite patriarchs. Joshua focuses on moving into the Promised Land and dividing the land among the 12 Israelite tribes. Judges relates the deliverance of the Israelites from enemies. Ruth is a snapshot of everyday life in the new country from the perspective of women.

When the Children of Israel entered the Promised Land, they set up the Tabernacle at Shiloh, an area of rolling hills. Israelite conquest of the Promised Land was characterized by many God-given successes. But, when the Israelites disobeyed God, they were defeated and encountered unnecessary struggles, i.e., as a result of the treaty with the Gibeonites. Often, Israelites seem clueless when trying to make the right decisions. Not much different from you and me, were they? Like the Israelites millennia ago, when we disobey God, we suffer the consequences.

****

Most of us rarely read the book of the godly Joshua. Nor do we hear many sermons on the book other than Joshua at the battle of Jericho, and Joshua averring that he and his house will serve God.

Have you thought about when you've succeeded in life and when you've failed? Most of us remember failures but rarely remember successes. In the 21st century, Christian failure isn't always associated with active disobedience to God, such as disobeying one of the 10 Commandments. Sometimes we fail because our undertaking isn't in the direction God wants us to go.

Can you correlate personal successes with obeying God and failures with ignoring God or outright disobeying him? One time when I had a monumental failure. I groaned in pain and cried. My head, chest, intestines, and muscles hurt. The incomprehensible part of this failure—at least to me at the time—was that I believed that I was obeying God. Have you been in a situation like that? What did you learn? I'm still not completely sure what I learned, but I am cautious about putting myself in the same situation again. Maybe that was what I was to learn.

Should I conclude that God is mean? Should I blame God for my failure? Believe me, for a while, I did that! I demanded that God make the pain go away. Do you blame God for your failures? Do you try to micromanage God?

Holding our behavior up to biblical direction and being accountable for it is hard and time-consuming. These actions are particularly hard when all we want to do is escape pain, self-reflection, self-awareness, and yes, even accountability.

On the other hand, we can't improve if we don't become "aware of" and "accountable for" our second-rate behavior. Sometimes we wall off pain without dealing with its cause. We ignore it, stuff it, and hope it will go away. Name a time or two when you did that? What are better ways of dealing with pain and shortcomings?

****

An aged Joshua called tribal leaders together under a giant oak tree near God's sanctuary at Shiloh. There, Joshua reminded them that God promised Abraham the land of Canaan. God fulfilled his promise. The Children of Israel conquered Canaan and lived in it. Now, they were "accountable to" guard and steward the land that God gave to them.

Joshua urged listeners to do all that was written in the Book of the Law of Moses. Primarily, to love God and put God first in their lives. Pointedly, Joshua told them not to mix or intermarry with the people remaining in Canaan, nor worship Canaanite gods. Joshua warned the Israelites that if they worshiped foreign gods, they would anger God.

In the first quarter of the 21st century, God gives humanity much the same message. Are you concerned that many Americans, like many Israelites, don't hold themselves accountable to God for this command? Most Christians have few thoughts about the faith of the individual they want to wed and spend their life with.

How easy is it to follow God using our willpower?

Israelites intermarried with Canaanites as early as their 2-3 generations in the Promised Land. God worship was compromised. Their children learned love of God from one parent and love of a false god (idol) from the other. With successive generations, the purity of God-worship was eroded further.

Saturday, I made dessert for a small dinner party. I used food coloring in white powdered sugar for the cake icing. The icing only required a small drop of food coloring to change the whiteness of the powdered sugar. The more food coloring, the darker the color of the cake icing.

The same process occurred in the Israelites in the Promised Land. Some accepted just a minute pagan belief, thinking the small amount wouldn't impact their adherence to God-worship. With each minute, acceptance purity of God worship was altered. The purity of the Israelites' worship of God was slowly eroded.

Joshua asked the Israelite elders to choose who they would serve, i.e., gods from beyond the River (Euphrates) or from Egypt or only God. Elders affirmed that they would serve God.

Then, Joshua said something astonishing to the listeners! Joshua told them that they weren't able to serve God. God was a holy and jealous God. God would punish them if they deserted him and served foreign gods. Despite Joshua's warning, the Israelite elders assured Joshua that they could serve only God.

Joshua wrote down the promises the Israelite elders made to God. He buried them and a copy of the Mosaic laws under oak trees and set a cairn of stones above them. Joshua told the elders that the stones were a "witness" against them; that the stones heard their promises. In essence, Joshua was holding the Israelites accountable for their promise to serve God.

Successive generations of Israelites who saw the stones should have remembered what they stood for—their promise to serve God. Much like Americans forget the significance of Plymouth Rock, Israelites forgot or ignored the rocks which signified their commitment to God.

The Bible asks 21st-century Christians the same question that Joshua asked the Israelites: "Are you willing to serve God or will you worship foreign gods?" For us, that means money, material goods, false prestige, etc. Like Joshua's tribal elders, we are quick to say that we will put away false gods and worship the true, living God. But are we? Do we? Think about the answers honestly. Name what you put before God.

****

Most 21st-century Christians know stories of Deborah's bravery and decisiveness (Judges chapters 3-5). The Bible described her as a prophet, judge, wife, and mother of Israel. Women use Deborah's actions to support an argument that women in Old Testament times were powerful heroines. Men use Deborah's life to argue that men in ancient times were accepting of women in leadership positions.

This episode occurred when Deborah told Barak that God commanded him to lead the Israelites against Canaanite King Jabin and his war commander Sisera (Judges 4:1-10).

Barak refused to command the Israelite troops in a battle against Sisera unless Deborah went with him. In a way, it seems like Barak saw Deborah as some sort of talisman. Barak's decision wasn't Deborah's preference, possibly not God's either.

Deborah's response to Barak was that she would go with him, but because of Barak's decision, he wouldn't get credit for killing Sisera. The credit would go to a woman. Apparently, Barak was okay with this plan. The Bible recorded no pushback from him.

How much is personal glory a factor in your decisions?

All of us make decisions daily in the home, workplace, or community. Some decisions are minor; they have little impact on our lives. Others are important and influence our life, including our testimony for Jesus for years to come. All our decisions aren't consistent with God's preference.

Decisions require us to select a course of action from different possibilities. A mental process, decision-making is influenced by our biases, reason, emotions, and memories.

Business gurus identified a process to aid in decision-making regardless of the setting. Notice I said that business gurus identified this model. As Christian's we know that God is bigger and wiser than any earthly discipline; nonetheless, this model can be used as you decide and plan.

The five steps of the decision-making model are:

1) Investigate the situation in detail. Don't miss or ignore any information that may impact the decision. This step is named "assessment." In a group setting, you may want to allow opinions to be anonymous. For example, on a church committee, members may be reluctant to disagree with an elder or pastor.

2) Generate good alternatives. Don't limit yourself to the first option you identify. Delve deep!

3) Explore implications that occur with each option. Don't forget to include financial and human costs.

4) Select the best solution to the problem. If you are making a family decision, don't ignore anyone's opinion, even children.

5) Decide how you will evaluate the outcome of any decision you make. How will you know if your decision resulted in success or failure? Choose the evaluation method before you start to implement the decision.

Do you think Barak evaluated his decision to require Deborah to go with him into battle with Sisera, or just forged ahead? If he had evaluated his decision before implementing it, maybe he would have changed his mind about needing Deborah's presence at the battle site. Some causes of poor decision-making include:

- Misidentifying the problem. Often, you solve a symptom of the problem but not the root cause of it.
- Not making any decision. Continuing as things currently operate or function is a decision.
- Letting biases, emotions, and memories influence a decision. Likely, you've heard in multiple committees the input, "We've tried that before and it didn't work," "We've always done it this way."
- Not including information and opinions of all stakeholders.
- Not communicating the decision to all persons who are impacted by it.

Having considered the business perspective on decision-making, we can't forget the most important factor for a Christian when deciding. Pray. Ask God not only which option he wants you to implement, but also if he wants you to be involved in thinking/deciding about the topic. For example, which Christian school to send your children to isn't a decision you need to make if God wants your child in public school

Before leaving this episode between Deborah and Barak, read Hebrews 11:17-40. The passage identifies standouts of the Hebrew faith beginning with Abraham. Several judges and Barak are highlighted in the list. Deborah's name isn't present. The only woman in the list is Rahab. The Hebrews' writer apparently thought that Barak had more faith than Deborah or contributed more to the outcome of the battle between King Jabin's army and the Israelites.

****

Jael's actions were central to Israelite success in the war against King Jabin in the Promised Land. Jael and her husband, Hebner, were Kenites. Hebner aligned himself with King Jabin and Commander Sisera. Kenites were metal workers. Likely, Hebner was involved in building King Jabin's 900 chariots. Hebner and Jael lived in tents in the Naphtali tribe's territory. In contrast to Hebner's, Jael's sympathies were with the Israelites.

Should a wife disagree substantially with her husband?

After Barak routed Sisera's army, Sisera fled on foot. He came to Jael's tent. Sisera felt secure there because of the alliance between Hebner and King Jabin. Jael went out to meet Sisera, told him not to be afraid, and welcomed him to her tent. There, Jael gave Sisera milk and encouraged him to lie down and sleep. Sisera instructed Jael to stand at her tent door. If anyone asked if Jael saw anyone pass by, Jael was to say "No."

While Sisera slept, Jael used a hammer to drive a tent peg through his temple into the ground. Jael killed Sisera. Soon afterward, Barak came to Jael's tent. Jael showed Barak Sisera's dead body. Deborah's words to Barak came true: a woman received the credit for killing Commander Sisera.

Although Jael's method of killing Sisera is gruesome, it demonstrates her resourcefulness. She used commonplace items around her tent. Sisera may have been suspicious if he saw a sword in Jael's tent. Seeing a tent peg and hammer elicited no comment or alarm—the Kenites lived in tents. Replacing and resecuring tent pegs were common occurrences.

Resourcefulness means you find quick and clever ways to solve a problem or overcome difficulties. You use what you have available rather than demand different, including more up-to-date equipment or additional staff. The saying, "work smarter, not harder," may be what resourceful individuals do.

Being resourceful is seeing potential in things or events that others consider useless—it's about finding an opportunity in a situation where other individuals don't see any.

Resourcefulness is a superlative attribute in the second quarter of the 21st century. We are experiencing a high rate of inflation. Few individuals can afford the same quality of life as a decade ago. Families, churches, and workplaces need resourceful individuals. The question is, how can you become that person?

Resourceful individuals need four basic traits: curiosity, creativity, optimism/sense of humor, and determination. If you have these traits, you can teach yourself to be resourceful, i.e., in the home, church, or workplace.

To become a resourceful individual and valuable to an employer, you will have to change some of your behaviors. Behavior change doesn't occur overnight and rarely without conscious thought. Most of us need to focus on thinking and acting in different ways, more creative/curious, etc., ways, until they become a habit. Despite the effort (cost), the benefit to you for being labeled resourceful in 21st-century society can't be understated.

There are four chief habits of resourceful individuals: First, they don't let challenges stop them. If a task can't be completed one way, they look for and find another way thus they seek never-tried solutions.

Second, they think outside the box. Resourceful individuals never let old ways of doing a task be the only way to do it. These are the individuals who look for more efficient and effective ways to do the same activity but at the same time make the best of what they have. They teach themselves new skills. They are willing to teach others new skills needed in the workplace or church.

Third, resourceful people are good communicators. They share new ideas with others but don't force their ideas on others. They aren't threatened when they need to ask for help.

Finally, resourceful individuals are the last to say, "We always did it that way." Often, they seem uninterested in past practices. They are the innovators.

Would you describe yourself as a resourceful person?

Have you ever wondered what Hebner thought when he returned to his tents and learned that his wife had killed his employer, i.e., the commander of King Jabin's army? Hopefully, Hebner didn't abuse Jael for it. Resourceful individuals aren't always accepted because they threaten the *status quo*. In this episode, perhaps Jael threatened the family's finances.

****

"Rash" is a label for the judge Jephthah. *Merriam-Webster's* dictionary describes "rash" as a lack of deliberation or caution and gives "a rash promise" as an example. Synonyms are hasty, impulsive, thoughtless, and even reckless. Let me explain why I apply this word to the judge Jephthah in this episode.

Three Israelite tribes settled east of the Jordan River: Reuben, Gad, and half the tribe of Manasseh. Collectively, this area was known as Gilead. Jephthah was a descendant of a man also named Gilead and a prostitute. He was reared in the family home until Gilead died. Then, his brothers expelled him from the home. Jephthah went to Tob, Syria, where he led a group of adventurers. Later, the Gileadites asked Jephthah to be their war commander.

Before Jephthah battled the Ammonites, he rashly promised God that if God gave him victory, then whatever came out from the doors of his house when he returned home, he would sacrifice to God as a burnt offering (Judges 11:30-31).

After victory over the Ammonites, Jephthah returned home. The first person out of his door was his only child, a beloved daughter (who the Bible didn't name). When Jephthah saw her, he was filled with anguish. In grief, he tore his clothes. Jephthah cried out to his daughter that she made him miserable. Jephthah blamed his daughter for his rash vow, refusing to take responsibility for it.

Unfortunately, Jephthah's attempt to manipulate God with his rash vow resulted in Jephthah killing his only child.

When something doesn't go our way or when we do something foolish, many Christians blame God—why did God let that happen? Rarely do these

Jesus-followers ask God for insights into why the outcome was suboptimal.

Have you ever acted rashly, that is, with undue haste? Have you ever taken an action or assumed a role that wasn't in God's plan for your life? Then, you expected God to give you success because you prayed about the topic.

To cover all bases—to secure what you considered an optimal outcome—did you attempt to bargain with God, i.e., "If you just allow me to get this position, all my decisions in the role will honor you." Did you ever consider that perhaps your action wasn't God's will?

A phrase in The Lord's Prayer, "Thy will be done," comes to mind when I read Jephthah's story. How often do we say, "Thy will be done," only to have a preconceived endpoint that is our will, not God's will?

Do you attempt to bargain with God?

Remember, God's promise, "For I know the plans I have for you…plans to prosper you and not to harm you" (Jeremiah 29:11). Do you believe this Bible verse?

While God plans to prosper, not harm us, our role is to diligently seek God's will. God won't always pull us from fires of our own making. Remember, God's teaching on consequences back in Chapter 1? In the depth of the pain of failure, it's hard not to blame someone, even God, for a failure. Yet, our consolation, our solace, is God's promise that

God's plan is to prosper our lives and to keep us from harm.

****

Naomi was an Israelite woman whose story is told in the book of Ruth. As her life unfolded, she didn't see God working for her good. The story begins with Naomi, her husband, and two sons relocating to Moab because of a famine in the Bethlehem region. Famine is a great shortage and most often refers to a shortage of food.

In the 21st-century United States, most individuals have little experience with famine. Food shortages are rarely a problem. Communities have food banks for residents who can't afford to purchase food. Unfortunately, food shortages occur in other parts of Earth, i.e., Africa, Asia, the Middle East, and South America.

The book of Revelation documents that shortages of food will occur at the end of the ages (Revelation 6:5-8). Famine from other than food exists. God said:

> "The days are coming," declares the Sovereign Lord, "when I will send a famine through the land—not a famine of food or a thirst for water, but a famine of hearing the words of the Lord. People will stagger from sea to sea and wander from north to east, searching for the word of the LORD, but they will not find it (Amos 8:11-12).

There are five aspects of humankind: physical, mental, social, psychological, and spiritual. Our spiritual self is our point of contact with God. Spiritual food is needed for our spiritual selves just as physical food is for our physical bodies. Without spiritual food we experience famine in our spirits.

In the 21st century, many Americans are starving spiritually but are unaware of their hunger. The solution to spiritual famine is God. Starving for God's Word isn't something to avoid. God wants us to hunger, to have an appetite for, his honesty, morality, and justice (Matthew 5:6).

What should we do about spiritual famine? How can we get filled when we hunger spiritually? We can't drive up to a gasoline station and fill our tank from the fuel hose. Nonetheless, God promises if we hunger and thirst for his righteousness, he will fill us.

What is God's food for your spirit?

Jesus said that he is the bread of life. If we come to Jesus, we will never hunger for spiritual food (John 6:35). Only Jesus can overcome our spiritual cravings as we live for God.

We can't eat (physically chew with our teeth and swallow) God's spiritual food, but we can consume it. Spiritual food is the Word of God. In the Bible, we find sustenance for our spiritual selves.

Another way we encounter, even ingest, spiritual food is by listening to Godly teachings. For example, *Right Now Media* provides videos on diverse biblical topics that can be watched to enhance a walk with Jesus. Some are short, others are longer. Some are a single episode and others are multi-episode. *YouTube* has Jesus-centered videos There are a plethora of Christian books in stores and available online in electronic format. A multitude of Jesus-centered podcasts are available.

Christians who consume Jesus should be conduits, taking him to the world, to individuals around them. We need to bear fruit for Jesus. Examples of bearing fruit include:

- love, willing the good of another,
- patience, or accepting the troublesome,
- **faithfulness in** dedication to a partner or friend,
- exhibiting self-control that restricts the havoc that the ego can cause.

Have you considered the myriad of ways you can transmit spiritual substance to others? The way you transmit spiritual substance to others is unique, just as you are unique. Further, the way you bear fruit at one stage of your life may be different than the way you bear fruit in another life stage. Importantly, bear fruit! Do it intentionally! Plan for and implement your plan for bearing fruit for Jesus.

Delving Deeper

Joshua told the Israelite leaders that they wouldn't be able to serve God totally. How could Joshua's statement be a self-fulfilling prophecy to the Israelites?

Read Deborah's song in Judges chapter 5. Which Israelite tribes/cities refused to fight with Barak? What did Sisera's mother think was the reason for her son's delay in returning home?

Are you resourceful? Identify individuals in your environment who you consider resourceful. How do they act differently from how you act?

Read Judges chapters 10-12, the story of Judge Jephthah. In Jephthah's interactions with Ephraimites, he seemed to be an impatient, even irritable, man. List some possible reasons that Jephthah attempted to make peace with the Ammonite king but treated his Ephraim brothers harshly. What occurred in between these two Bible episodes that could have influenced his thinking?

Ponder spiritual famine. Can you identify a time in your life when you hungered for God's Word? How did you feel? What was happening at the time? What did you do? Alternatively, describe a time you didn't care if you had God's spirit or not. Were other happenings in your life more important? Compare the times. Did you learn anything?

Chapter 5

KINGS & QUEENS

The classic song "Kings & Queens"[11] by Mat Kearny is about taking on the world and feeling the ruler of it. It's about having the power to do anything you want while finding your place in the world. This mindset reflects the Israelite kings and queens described in Chapter 5. You will note that they are a diverse group.

After the Israelites lived in the Promised Land for up to 400 years, they wanted a king to lead them in battle against foreign aggressors. Israelites believed that if they used a type of lottery to choose the king, the man would be God's choice.

Saul, from the tribe of Benjamin, was chosen by the lottery as the first monarch of the Israelites. King David, the most loved king in Israelite history, succeeded King Saul. David's son, King Solomon, ascended to the throne after King David. Solomon's reign was the "golden age" of Israelite history. During King Solomon's reign, God's Temple was built.

After Solomon's death, the 10 northern tribes (Israel, Northern Kingdom) separated from the Israelite monarchy. They established Samaria as their capital city. Judah remained as the only tribe in the Davidic kingdom (Judah, Southern Kingdom). Jerusalem was its capital. At times, Benjamin aligned with Israel and other times with Judah. One Queen, Athaliah, ruled Judah.

Stories from approximately 3000 years ago, set in the Middle East, offer insights for Christian life in 21st-century Westernized countries.

****

During King Saul's reign, the Philistines were a persistent Israelite enemy. In one campaign, King Saul camped under a pomegranate tree. The Hebrew word for pomegranate tree and its fruit comes from *râmon*[5,] which means "to exalt" or "lift up."

Perhaps, Saul had "exalt" in mind when he camped under the *râmon*[5] tree. As the first king over Israel, Saul knew his behavior and choices were scrutinized by supporters and detractors alike. By camping under a tree that meant "exalt," Saul reminded Israelites that God exalted him to the position of king.

We live in a "promote yourself" world. Do you promote—exalt—yourself? Each time we achieve something, i.e., good grade at school, achievements in the workplace we tell others on social media. We brag about our accomplishments to other members of the family.

Self-exaltation is the antithesis of what God wants from us. God doesn't think that degrees, a prestigious job title, a big house, high income, or popularity are valuable. God created Earth and the cosmos. The amount of money in our 401K is minute in God's estimation.

Jesus said those who exalt themselves will be humbled (Matthew 23:12). Our criteria for exalting ourselves and others are different from God's criteria. We need to get with God's program.

How can you change your self-exalting behavior? Do you even want to do so?

Here's who God says should be exalted:

In your relationships with one another, have the same mindset as Christ Jesus: Who, being in very nature God, did not consider equality with God something to be used to his own advantage; rather, he made himself nothing by taking the very nature of a servant, being made in human likeness.

And being found in appearance as a man, he humbled himself by becoming obedient to death—even death on a cross! Therefore God exalted him to the highest place and gave him the name that is above every name, that at the name of Jesus every knee should bow, in heaven and on earth and under the earth, and every tongue acknowledge that Jesus Christ is Lord, to the glory of God the Father (Philippians 2:5-11).

God has lifted, or wants to lift, each of us out of the despair and draining numbness of our daily lives. God wants us to live exposed to him, his purpose, and will for our lives. Have you allowed God to exalt you by giving you his name, i.e., Christian? If you are a Christian, how can you live so that you continually exalt God—rather than yourself?

Instead of exalting ourselves, God instructs us to humble ourselves. When we are humble, we act modestly, respectfully, unassumingly, and have a spirit of deference and submission.

Writing in *Forbes*, Jeff Boss[12] noted that humble people get a bad rap, yet humble individuals are the best people to work with. He identified the habits of humble individuals. Most agree with the Bible's perspective on humility. According to Boss,[12] humble people:

1) Try to learn about the situation before speaking or acting.

2) Are more likely to assist friends than are prideful individuals.

3) Make decisions on the basis of shared purpose rather than self-interest.

4) Know their self-worth so they don't need to

show others how much they know.

5) Start sentences with "You" rather than "I."

6) Enlist help from others, i.e., often Jesus allowed disciples to generate solutions.

7) Take time to say, "Thank you."

Over time, King Saul ceased all effort to be humble, and obey and honor God. In response, God took the Holy Spirit from King Saul. God replaced it with an evil spirit that tormented Saul (1 Samuel 16:14). Eventually, Saul and three sons (Johnathan, Abinadab, and Malki-Shua) were killed in a battle with the Philistines. The Philistines cut off Saul's head and fastened his body and the bodies of his sons to a city wall. Saul's self-exaltation and disregard for God's perspective resulted in tragedy for Israel's first king.

****

After King Saul was killed, David became king over the Israelites. The Bible introduces David to readers when he was a boy. Alone, the boy David confronted and killed a giant Philistine soldier, Goliath, using a slingshot and stones (1 Samuel 17:48-49). Subsequently, David was married to King Saul's youngest daughter, Michal. King Saul initiated the marriage between David and Michal as a way to capture and kill David.

In one episode, King Saul sent men to David and Michal's house. Michel learned of her father's plot. Michel lowered David from a window with a rope, thus allowing him to escape King Saul's murderous plan.

Over the next 8-10 years, David was on the run from King Saul. During that time, David didn't attempt to retrieve Michal so she could be with him. David married two other women. King Saul arranged a marriage for Michel with a close ally. Perhaps David was grateful to Michal, but he wasn't loyal to the royal princess who saved his life.

Michal loved David (1 Samuel 19:28); however, nowhere did the Bible record that David loved Michal. Can you imagine how lonely Michal felt at David's abandonment and at being a pawn in her father's ploys?

The Bible tells us how to think when we feel lonely. Christians are to live beyond their feelings, knowing God helps them even in their loneliness. Here are some of God's assurances when we face loneliness.

- You are never alone. You always have three companions: God the Father, God the Son, and God the Holy Spirit. God never leaves you, even if family members do—"I will not leave you as orphans" (John 14:18).
- God sets the lonely in families (Psalm 68:6). He is a father to the fatherless, a defender (even husband) to widows.
- Don't be anxious about anything (Philippians 4:6-7). Turn to God. Tell God your feelings and requests to include, "God, I feel lonely." God promises that he will give you his peace, even when your heart is broken.

- Don't fear even though you walk through a valley shadowed with evil, that is, even though you live in the 21st century. God is always there protecting you. Nothing can separate you from God's love (Romans 8:39).

Dr. David Jeremiah[13] suggested three strategies for Christians to use to overcome loneliness. First, embrace intimacy with God. God knows we need to be in a relationship. At times, feeling lonely is a gift from God. The feeling allows us to reach out to God. Remember King David's prayer to God, "Turn to me and be gracious to me, for I am lonely and afflicted" (Psalm 25:16). You can pray the same prayer to God.

Second, allow God's word to fill your heart and mind. Living with and for Jesus requires us to get into and remain in fellowship with God. That means reading the Bible and applying it to our lives.

Third, activate your network of Christian friends. Bruce and I live many hours from our families. Sometimes, particularly around holidays, we feel lonely. By God's grace, we found a Bible-believing church with individuals who want to be our family.

The Bible contains no evidence that Michal engaged in any strategy to reproach King David. Instead, she became a bitter woman whose criticism further alienated David from her (2 Samuel 6:20-23). Heartbreaking situation, isn't it?

When I think about King David and Michal, I am reminded of a verse from the song "Jesus Walked this Lonesome Valley."[14]

We must walk this lonesome valley.
We have to walk it by ourselves.
O, nobody else can walk it for us.
We have to walk it by ourselves.

Although nobody else can walk our valley for us, we don't have to walk through the valley alone. God wants to walk it with us. David seems to understand that God walked with him. I am less sure that Michal had this same understanding.

Before leaving the episode on King David and Michal, let's remember that the imperfect King David was a man after God's own heart. When King David separated himself from God by sinning and became aware of his sin, David promptly confessed it. God forgave him.

How can Christians reach perfection here on Earth?

Today, in the 21st century, we sin and separate ourselves from God. When we do, we have a choice. We can remain separate from God (alone)—or we can tell God we are sorry for what we did. We can repent as King David did. It's our decision to re-establish a relationship with God, just as it was Michal's decision to re-establish her relationship with King David or further her separation from him.

****

I'd really like to be wise. Wouldn't you? This entry recounts two episodes in the life of King Solomon, the wisest man in the Old Testament. The first episode describes how Solomon became wise. Another series of verses documents how Solomon lost his wisdom. We can use these episodes and other Bible verses to get and keep wisdom.

While making an offering to God, King Solomon had a vision. God told Solomon to ask him for whatever Solomon wanted. God would give it to Solomon (1 Kings 3:5-9). Wouldn't you love God to make you an offer like that?

King Solomon asked God for a discerning heart to govern the Israelites and to distinguish right from wrong. God was pleased with King Solomon's request (1 Kings 3:10-15). God promised that Solomon would have no equal among kings; thus, God averred that Solomon would have the wisdom and discernment he requested. God promised that as long as Solomon walked in his ways, God would give him not only wisdom but long life, riches, and honor.

We wish that King Solomon had been totally dedicated to God all the days of his life, but that didn't happen. God commanded that the Israelites to not intermarry with individuals from foreign nations. Nonetheless, King Solomon married many foreign women, i.e., Egyptian, Ammonite, Edomite, and Moabite women. King Solomon had 700 wives of royal birth and 300 concubines. He loved many of them.

Solomon's wives led him from God-worship to worship of additional gods, such as Molek, Ba'al, and Chemosh. Solomon set up temples and altars on hills east of Jerusalem for his wives' gods.

God became angry because King Solomon turned his heart from him. God told Solomon that because Solomon refused to keep his laws and decrees, he would rend the Israelite kingdom from Solomon's line. Yet, because of God's love for King David, God wouldn't tear the entire kingdom from Solomon. Further, God wouldn't take the Israelite kingdom from Solomon but from his son. God would allow Solomon's son one tribe and the city of Jerusalem to rule.

Solomon's sin and disobedience resulted in consequences just as Adam and Eve's sin in the Garden of Eden resulted in consequences. Our sin results in consequences to include to any discernment we have.

Most 21st-century individuals want wisdom. Wisdom is astuteness, insight, perception, and judgment. Back home in rural Pennsylvania, we called wisdom "good sense;" that may be the best definition of wisdom that I've heard. It goes well beyond merely knowing facts.

No one is born wise. A person with wisdom needs knowledge, but not all knowledgeable individuals are wise. Wisdom and knowledge are different, even though the Bible says that fear of the Lord is the beginning of both:

> The fear of the Lord is the beginning of wisdom, and knowledge of the Holy One is understanding (Proverbs 9:10).

The fear of the Lord is the beginning of knowledge, but fools despise wisdom and instruction (Proverbs 1:7).

Don't equate wisdom with intelligence or education. The first third of the 21st century United States has a larger proportion of educated individuals than any society in history, but how many of them are truly wise?

Let me give you an example of education without wisdom. Individuals with multiple college degrees are highly educated and knowledgeable, at least in a specialty area. Those same individuals may not be able to distinguish between what is a right and a wrong act. Nor can they formulate a logical argument because they have trouble seeing relationships between pieces of data/information. They aren't wise. Disobeying God isn't wise.

Humankind's wisdom differs from Godly wisdom. Human wisdom wants what society identifies as success, regardless of whether that success is right or wrong. Human wisdom is social acuity (sharpness). In contrast, Godly wisdom knows that a life not centered on God isn't satisfying, nor does it reflect true wisdom. That type of life isn't right with God; thus, it can't be right with others in our home, church, workplace, or community.

We break out of the bonds of human limitations of wisdom when we embrace God and his wisdom, when we put God in his proper place in our lives. How can our perception of wisdom change from a societal one to a Godly one?

How could your life improve if you had Godly wisdom?

How do we get to be a wise Christian? The Bible has a really easy answer. Ask God for wisdom! Here's how James put it, "If any of you lacks wisdom, he should ask God, who gives generously to all without finding fault, and it will be given him" (James 1:5). Because I am a woman, I replace the masculine pronouns with feminine ones, but the instruction is the same.

Notice, God, through James, doesn't conclude that you are dumb, i.e., that you should have all this knowledge. After all, it's in the Bible. You can read it and figure it out. No, God doesn't find fault with us. God wants us, his children, to ask him for what we want, including wisdom.

We grow in Godly wisdom when we internalize God's precepts and instructions. These we learn by reading the Bible and hearing it. Equally important, we must ponder and ask, "How does this word, phrase, clause, verse apply to my life today?" James admonished Christians to do what the Bible says (James 1:22-25).

Do not merely listen to the word and so deceive yourselves. Do what it says.

Anyone who listens to the word but does not do what it says is like someone who looks at his face in a mirror and, after looking at himself, goes away and immediately forgets what he looks like.

But whoever looks intently into the perfect law that gives freedom and continues in it—not forgetting what they have heard but doing it—they will be blessed in what they do.

****

After Solomon died, his son, Rehoboam, became king. That's when the Israelite monarchy split into the Northern and Southern Kingdoms. The two kingdoms were almost constantly at war. This episode of the Divided Kingdoms is about an "insult" between the two kings.

King Amaziah of the Southern Kingdom challenged King Joash (Jehoash) of the Northern Kingdom to battle. King Joash sent a message back to King Amaziah in the form of a parable:

> A thistle in Lebanon sent a message to a cedar in Lebanon…..you are arrogant and proud. But stay at home! Why ask for trouble and cause your own downfall and that of Judah also? (2 Chronicles 25:17-19).

The opening line of the message from King Joash to King Amaziah is the key to its meaning. In it, King Joash of the Northern Kingdom named Israel a cedar and Judah a thistle. Characteristics of thistles versus cedar trees make the parable's point. Thistles are found in abandoned fields and ditches. Thistles grow as weeds and are rarely taller than about three feet. In contrast, cedars were the largest and most majestic trees in the Middle East. Cedars are evergreen trees, beautiful in summer and winter. The cedar grows to 120 feet tall. It takes centuries to produce a majestic cedar tree.

Calling a nation a thistle is an insult. An insult is a slight, a slur, an affront, rudeness, or even a form of abuse. 21st-century Western society is a verbal society. Rarely is physical aggression used to settle status issues. Instead, insults are used. Insults reduce the status of the target while raising the status of the insulter. In this instance, the insulter was the Northern Kingdom. The target of the insult was the Southern Kingdom (Judah).

In an internet post on the psychology of insults, Barber[15] noted that often insults are motivated by anger or insecurity about the insulter's own status. Sometimes insults are reactive, a response to a real or imagined slight from another.

Frequently, insults reference a target's social status, ancestry, intelligence, or membership in an outgroup. In the 21st-century USA, Christians are an "outgroup" and a common target of insults by the majority culture. For example, at this time in the United States, the Speaker of the House of Representatives of the federal government is an avowed Christian. He is insulted for his Christian beliefs, words, and actions.

Insults aren't a new behavior, but they seem to have grown in number in the 21st century. Social media is a perfect environment for insulting others. It provides a shield of anonymity and absence of consequences to the insulter. Effective communities, i.e., churches, workplaces, etc., maintain group solidarity by eliminating insults to each other.

The Bible, written thousands of years ago, gave advice on how to respond to insults: "A soft answer turns away wrath, but harsh words stir up anger" (Proverbs 51:1).

When King Amaziah challenged King Joash to battle, what would have happened if King Joash returned a soft answer? Likely, there would have been no battle between the two kingdoms. No men would have been killed.

A soft answer leaves the aggressor with nowhere to go; there is no escalation of the conflict. Perhaps, the aggressor even feels embarrassed and humbled, rather than superior. Another Hebrew proverb is: "Whoever keeps his mouth and tongue keeps himself out of trouble" (Proverbs 21:23).

The last time you were insulted, how did you respond? How did you feel?

We want to be a Jesus-follower not only with what comes out of our mouths but what is in our hearts. Thinking hateful thoughts, thinking insults, but not saying them, is control, not love, as Jesus commands. Our hearts and minds must align with Jesus' command to love.

The Bible, the self-help book for 21st-century Christians, gives wise advice for dealing with insults. My go-to verse is:

> Do not repay evil for evil or reviling for reviling, but on the contrary, bless, for to this you were called, that you may obtain a blessing (1 Peter 3:9).

In this life you will be insulted. You may feel inadequate when you hear the nasty things said about you, even to you. Below are some suggestions that will help you deal with insults.

1) Recognize what you feel, i.e., angry, inadequate.

2) If you feel angry or hurt at being insulted, tell God how you feel. Ask him for a tender heart, a forgiving heart, toward the insulter.

3) Remember how much God forgave you. Once we are aware of how much God forgave us, it's easier to forgive others, pray for them, and not respond to their insult with an insult.

4) Place a copy of this Bible verse on your bathroom mirror (or where you will see it daily). Read it every morning as you start your day and every evening as you end your day:

> You must rid yourself of all things such as these: put away anger, rage, malice, slander, and filthy language from your mouth (Colossians 3:8).

This verse isn't a suggestion. It's a directive from God. Notice the word "must."

****

Queen Athaliah, the only female ruler over the Israelites (841-835 BCE), ruled the Southern Kingdom from Jerusalem. Athaliah was most likely the daughter of King Ahab and Queen Jezebel of Israel (Northern Kingdom). Her marriage to King Jehoram of Judah was political; it formed an alliance between the two Israelite kingdoms. The marriage was designed to stop wars between the two Israelite kingdoms.

After King Jehoram (Ataliah's husband) died, their son Ahaziah became king. When Athaliah learned that her son, King Ahaziah, was dead, she killed King Ahaziah's children, her own grandchildren. With that act, Athaliah thought the Davidic line of kings ended. She was wrong. One grandson, Josiah, survived and later became king of Judah.

Like her ancestors, Queen Athaliah worshiped Ba'al. She built a temple to Ba'al in Jerusalem. After seven years as queen, Athaliah was killed by her subjects. Neither God nor Judah rejected Athaliah because she was a woman. The reason was Athaliah's excess pride, which led to her ruthless behavior.

Most of us living in the 21st century don't believe we are filled with pride. In particular, Christians want to think of themselves as just the opposite of proud, that is, as humble. Pride was the first sin in the Garden of Eden. Pride is the most serious sin and undergirds almost all other sins. We grew up reciting the proverb, "Pride goes before destruction" (Proverbs 16:18).

The Devil doesn't stand before us with a banner saying, "You are proud." How can we tell if pride is motivating our behavior? Dr. Natasha Penny[16] posted statements on Hope Bible Church, Canada, that if we answer in the affirmative, can indicate that we are proud. Some statements are listed below. Check the ones that apply to you.

- I feel special about my:
  - _____ house
  - _____ physical gifts, i.e., tennis, jogging
  - _____ spiritual gifts, i.e., teacher, prophet
  - _____ looks
  - _____ intellect
  - _____ education
  - _____ job
  - _____ car
- _____ I regularly compare myself with others.
- _____ I want people to be impressed by me.
- _____ I'm competitive.
- _____ I feel deserving. I deserve what I have.

Don't neglect to do this inventory. I have work to do. Maybe you do also.

God doesn't want to hurt our pride. God wants us to destroy our pride.

Being prideful isn't a characteristic that we have at one point in our life and then it goes away. For example, pride doesn't go away with age; we don't grow out of it. The struggle with pride is

110

lifelong. Born-again believers contend with pride in themselves.

Ways you can deal with pride in your life:[16]

1) Ask God to show you where you are prideful and to give you a holy hatred for your pride.. Then, ask God to help you act differently.

2) Confess your pride to God, being as specific as possible. You can use the above list to identify specific situations for focus in your life. Go through the list and ask God to help you with each item. You may even want to apologize to colleagues that you wronged secondary to being prideful. Apologizing to another individual is hard, but it helps to firm up new behavior.

3) Ask trusted friends to hold you accountable for prideful moments or events in your life. When friends hold us accountable for our pride, we often become defensive. As much as possible, accept a friend's input.

4) Scripture (1 Peter 5:6) tells us that we are to humble ourselves. Being humble is a decision that we make. We decide to think and act differently. Then we do it. Remember Leon Festinger's[6] theory of Cognitive Dissonance?

Before we leave this section on pride, I want to emphasize that individual pride is deceptive. I felt convicted by,

> All a man's ways seems innocent to him,
> but motives are weighed by the Lord
> (Proverbs 16:2).

That's me. Frequently, I rationalize that I don't do anything wrong. Certainly, I don't act pridefully. Wrong, Wrong, Wrong! Most of us cringe when we realize that God knows the origin of all our actions. God knows our motives and our heart. God knows those acts that are the result of pride. Those acts are as filthy rags to God.

Delving Deeper

How would an individual after God's own heart act in the 21st century? Have you ever described anyone that way? What did their behavior look like? What actions do you need to take in your life to have others name you an individual after God's heart?

Study King David's life. Find a place where he sinned. What did David do when he became aware of his sin? What lesson should we learn from this point in King David's life that can apply to our life in the 21st century?

How often do you, as an individual, need to confess your sins to God? How can confession of sins become routine and lose its meaning?

If you were told to ask for whatever you wanted and it would be given to you, what would you ask for?

How was Queen Athaliah's murder of her grandchildren viewed as particularly evil by the people of Judah? Dig deep into Queen Athaliah's life and reign. What other descriptions show her pride?

Chapter 6

FREEDOM IS A VOICE

Freedom from personal and societal chains has inspired individuals for centuries. The song "Freedom is a Voice" isn't only a physical or external condition but a powerful force within individuals.[17] True freedom requires determination, perseverance, and a strong spirit. This chapter encompasses messages from prophets, perhaps the first freedom fighters, rather than actions of war leaders, judges, or kings.

Prophecy is words spoken by inspiration. Israelite prophets were inspired by God. They gave two types of messages, foretelling and forthtelling. USA Christians are more familiar with foretelling, predictions of what will occur at a future time. Examples are Isaiah's prophecy about the Messiah and Revelation's prophecy on end times.

Forthtelling is speaking out (forth) God's word to those whom God desired to hear it. In the 21st century, much prophecy is forthtelling; yet Bible students know more about prophets' foretelling than forthtelling messages.

Elijah was the most famous prophet of God in the Northern Kingdom and arguably in the Old Testament. When Ahab (874-853 BCE) became ruler of the Northern Kingdom, Ahab married Jezebel, who worshiped Ba'al. Queen Jezebel built temples to Ba'al throughout the Northern Kingdom and consecrated priests to serve Ba'al.

In an encounter with Ahab, Elijah challenged Ba'al's prophets to identify which deity—Ba'al or God—would answer his prophet(s) by igniting a sacrificial fire. Ba'al's prophets couldn't persuade Ba'al to set fire to their offering. They prayed to Ba'al for hours. In contrast, the first time Elijah asked God to light the sacrifice, fire consumed the offering. Onlookers fell down and worshiped God. Elijah commanded them to slaughter Ba'al's prophets. Approximately 400 priests were killed.

King Ahab was at the sacrifice. He reported the happening to Queen Jezebel. She sent a message to Elijah declaring that she would have him killed within the next 24 hours. In terror, Elijah fled Samaria. He ran south to an area around Beersheba in Judah, over 100 miles.

Elijah was disheartened. What should have been a victory for God and Elijah turned into Elijah fleeing for his life. Queen Jezebel persecuted Elijah for his righteousness (right behavior). Religious persecution is the mistreatment of an individual or a group of individuals in response to their religious beliefs or affiliations.

Christianity is the most persecuted faith in the world.

Persecution is rampant in the Bible. In Egypt, the Israelites were persecuted because of their nationality and religion. Throughout the Bible, women lived as secondary citizens, a form of persecution. Jesus was persecuted by Pharisees because of his teachings. Paul was persecuted by Gentiles and Jews because he was a missionary for Jesus.

Sometimes religious persecution is blatant, while at other times subtle, but it's always harmful. 21st-century Christians can learn from this Old Testament story of Queen Jezebel persecuting Elijah.

About 12 years ago, in a home group, I offered that I didn't know if I was being persecuted in the workplace because I was a Christian versus persecuted because of my personality and behavior. Others agreed that they had the same difficulty.

What about you? Have you pondered the differences between the two—persecution because of your personality/behavior versus persecution for your Christian witness? God alone knows what is in the heart of persecutors, what motivates their actions. Whatever the reason for persecutors' actions, our response should be the same.

Below are some questions and answers on persecution based on the Bible direction:

Who will be persecuted? Godly individuals will be persecuted. Few men were godlier than Saint Paul, yet he was stoned multiple times for his witness for Jesus.

Will Christians be persecuted in the 21st century? Jesus said that Christians will be delivered to courts and flogged and dragged before governors and kings for Jesus' sake (Matthew 10:17). These seemingly bad situations are an opportunity to witness for Jesus.

Jesus said that if Christians were of this world, then the world would love them, but because Christians aren't like worldly individuals, the world hates them (John 15:19). A servant never gets better treatment than his/her master (John 15:20). The world persecuted Jesus. The world will persecute you if you follow Jesus. Notice there is no endpoint for Jesus' prophetic statement. Expect to be persecuted for your faith.

What should Christian's feel/think when they are persecuted? The answer is—you should feel blessed. Jesus said blessed are those who are persecuted, reviled, and talked evilly about for his sake (Matthew 5:10-12).

How long will persecution last? When will persecution end? Christians will be persecuted until the Rapture occurs or the Christian dies.

Will there be a reward for those who suffer persecution for Jesus? Yes! You will receive eternal life, a great reward, and a hundred-fold reward in Heaven (Matthew 5:12; Mark 10:30).

These words on persecution spoken 2000 years ago by Jesus and the early church fathers are applicable in the 21st century. In 2000 years, the environment for Jesus' followers hasn't improved.

****

Isaiah was another famous Israelite prophet. Christians know Isaiah primarily because he foretold the coming of the Messiah. Isaiah lived in Jerusalem during the reigns of Kings Uzziah, Jotham, Ahaz, and Hezekiah. Isaiah wrote a little-known wisdom poem, the Poem of the Plowman, to the Northern Kingdom (Isaiah 28:24-29). Although a poem, it was also a parable. The Poem affirmed that God's discipline to each of us is related to our circumstances, that is, not everyone receives the same level and type of discipline from God.

A problem for 21st-century Westernized individuals is that the Poem of the Plowman doesn't sound like a poem. We're used to rhyming or at least a certain tempo (pace, rhythm) in a poem. Translated Hebrew poems don't give either. As a result, we don't memorize Hebrew poetry even when it's in the Bible.

The poem's background is important, or should be important, to 21st-century Christian's because it mirrors the first decades of the 21st century. At this time in Israelite history, Israelite leaders scoffed at God. They asked: Who is God to try to teach us (Isaiah 28:9)? Are we babies? Are we newly weaned children? No! We have grown and evolved as people.

These rulers of the Northern Kingdom believed they didn't need God's specific instruction. They boasted they entered a covenant with death and the grave (Isaiah 28:15). If a foreign nation invaded them, they wouldn't be touched.

Leaders believed they didn't need God. Sound familiar?

When I read these words of Israelite leaders, I marveled at how humans 3000 years ago could be so brazen. Then, I thought about the opinions of some 21st-century writers, including theologians, i.e., there is no God; all gods are equal; gods were created by humans because humans needed something to believe in greater than themselves; and humankind evolved from lower-order creatures.

In the 21st-century United States, individuals have much the same attitude as Northern Kingdom citizens. They believe that life in a powerful nation protects them from external threats. They thought that Mosaic scripture and prophets/pastors' teachings were of little value.

Here is Isaiah's (28:24-29) Poem of the Plowman:

> When a farmer plows for planting, does he plow continually? Does he keep on breaking up and working the soil? When he has leveled the surface, does he not sow caraway and scatter cumin? Does he not plant wheat in its place, barley in its plot, and spelt in its field?

His God instructs him and teaches him the right way. Caraway is not threshed with a sledge, nor is the wheel of a cart rolled over cumin; caraway is beaten out with a rod, and cumin with a stick. Grain must be ground to make bread; so one does not go on threshing it forever.

All this also comes from the Lord Almighty.

The Poem of the Plowman is about discipline and how God disciplines his creation. Discipline is training that corrects, molds, and perfects our mental ability and moral character. Because God loves all humankind, God disciplines Christians and non-Christians.

Just as different types of seeds need different types of planting, cultivating, and harvesting, different individuals need different disciplines. God disciplines individuals he loves (Proverbs 3:12; Revelation 3:19).

A humorous Israelite proverb on discipline is "Whoever loves correction loves discipline, but he who hates correction is stupid" (Proverbs 12:1). When I read the proverb in a commentary, I didn't believe that the Bible would say someone is "stupid." I checked the verse in my NIV Bible. Yes, the Bible really does say that an individual who hates correction/discipline is stupid.

Most of my life, I believed that God has a set, i.e., consistent, constant, stereotypical, response to a sin. Given the words in the Poem of the Plowman, I was wrong. God considers the circumstances in the sinner's life when he disciplines. As a farmer uses different techniques to prepare soil and sow seeds, God uses different discipline techniques. A mother who steals food so her hungry children can eat receives a different discipline level from God than a woman who steals for wicked reasons.

Carefully, God selects discipline suited for a person's sins/needs. God uses the lightest possible touch that is appropriate. God never allows his discipline to be greater than an individual can bear. God directs fathers not to exasperate children, but rather to bring them up in the training and discipline of the Lord (2 Timothy 1:7). In the same way, God doesn't exasperate his children. God disciplines us so we grow to know and love him, not to feel punished.

We heed God's discipline to learn the way to eternal life. The opposite is also true. If we don't heed God's discipline, we go astray. Importantly, we don't have to engage with God's discipline in our own strength. The Holy Spirit gives Christians power, love, and self-discipline (2 Timothy 1:7). After the Holy Spirit indwells Christians, the Holy Spirit facilitates learning God's ways (discipline).

****

We remember Hosea because, at God's direction, Hosea married Gomer, an adulterous woman. Hosea's interactions with Gomer are a metaphor for the adultery between Northern Kingdom citizens and the idols they worshiped.

Because Hosea lived among the northern tribes, he knew their pride and perversions. Hosea averred that Israel's disloyalty to God and idol worship were spiritual adultery. Hosea exhorted the nation to do three things: a) stop sinning by no longer worshiping idols, b) ask God to forgive their sins, and c) return to God (Hosea 14:1-2). As Hosea accepted Gomer back into his home after Gomer repented of adultery, God will accept the Israelites back into love and care after they repent of idolatry.

God said that if Israel repented, God would cause the Northern Kingdom to blossom like the lily and the grapevine, grow like a cedar of Lebanon, have the splendor of an olive tree, smell like a cedar tree, flourish like grain, and be as famous as wine from Lebanon (Hosea 14:5-9).

God implores each of us in the 21st century to do the same—stop worshiping idols, repent, and return to God! If we do, God will heal us, i.e., we will blossom, grow, flourish, and smell fragrant to others.

Worship of idols is prohibited by the Ten Commandments, but these commandments were given 3500 years ago. Why is idolatry still talked about in 21st-century America? After all, westernized individuals don't worship manmade images as they did in the Bible. We are more knowledgeable and sophisticated than that.

The answer to the "why" question is that we idolize celebrities and worship achievements, i.e., money, job title, house, education, and beauty. We put people, achievements, and objects before God. They become our idols. Individuals who worship idols give up faithfulness to God (Jonah 2:8); they become idolaters.

After church last Sunday, we went to a sandwich shop for lunch. It was in a small mall that included a large grocery store. The grocery store parking spaces were filled. I wondered how many of these individuals did their grocery shopping rather than attend church. Was time their idol? Did some put personal time before honoring God at the Sunday morning church service?

So what if we don't obey the first and second commandments? Does God really care? The answer is a little-known verse in Psalms, "The sorrows of those will increase who run after other gods" (Psalm 16:4). According to the Bible, humans need no god except God (Exodus 20:3). They are to guard against idolatry and flee from it (1 John 5:21; 1 Corinthians 10:14).

Idol worship creeps into our lives slowly. If we went from following Jesus to where we are today (on a God-idol worship continuum) in one step, we would be appalled at the distance. But when the movement occurs an inch at a time (incrementally), we don't realize we are moving.

Fleeing idolatry begins with recognition and awareness. In our lavish 21st-century society, it's easy to put many things before God. We aren't aware that our worship is reordered. God is positioned lower on the list.

Here is an activity for you: Make a list of what you love, adore, and can't do without. Is God on the list? If so, where does God appear on it? First or somewhere after other items? If God isn't first on your list, consider making some priority changes.

Making priority changes is tough. Ask God to help you put him first in your life. Then, intentionally change your thoughts or actions. Remember the anecdote of individuals shopping on Sunday morning rather than being at church? That is an example of a skewed priority list that needs to be changed. Most behavioral changes have to be intentional. We must want to make them.

Is the root cause of idolatry the worship of self?

When I thought about idolatry and 21st-century society, the prohibition against making graven images got my attention. Increasingly, I see individuals taking pictures of themselves. Then, they post these pictures on social media and social places. They are idolizing themselves. Is the 21st-century society's trend of "selfies" the graven images of millennia ago? Reflect on the time spent making and posting self-images in comparison to time spent with God. We worship ourselves!

****

Good King Josiah instituted religious reform in Jerusalem (2 Kings chapter 22). As God's Temple was restored, a Book of Law was found. The book was read to King Josiah. It detailed that God's anger would come on the Israelites as a result of their rejection of God. King Josiah was devastated by what he heard. He instructed five of his top advisors to go to a prophet and find out what would happen to him and the Israelites.

They went to the prophetess, Huldah, who lived in Jerusalem (2 Kings 22:14-30). Huldah was a contemporary of the prophets Jeremiah and Habakkuk. Perhaps King Josiah's delegation thought that a woman would give a softer, or more favorable, interpretation of God's pending wrath. In reality, both prophets and prophetesses declared God's exact words without interpretation. All prophets (male or female) would give the same interpretation.

After the delegation from King Josiah showed Huldah the Book of Law, they asked her what was going to happen. Her response wasn't encouraging. God was angry! All curses in the Book of Law were going to come on Jerusalem, but they wouldn't until after King Josiah died because his heart was contrite.

God got angry (2 Kings 17:18). Jesus got angry (Matthew 21:12-13; Mark 11:15-18; John 2:13-22). Anger isn't always a sin, but sometimes it is. In Greek, the language the New Testament, there are two words for anger. One means "passion, energy," and the other means "agitated, boiling."

All 21st-century Christians get angry from time to time. Anger is an emotion that occurs as readily in us as love, compassion, irritation, etc. Being honest means differentiating between godly and ungodly anger. Many individuals trick themselves into thinking that anger is godly when it's not.[18]

Anger issues take a toll on the person's health, relationships, and overall quality of life! Anger results in physical changes in the body. In the short term, adrenaline release (which occurs when we are angry) causes an increased heart rate, increased blood pressure, and muscle tension. The long-term effects of intense and prolonged anger are debilitating. They include headaches, anxiety, high blood pressure, and increased risk of heart disease.

It takes at least 20 minutes for the nervous system to re-regulate and the body to calm down and return to normal after an anger episode. Thinking about the anger incident can cause another adrenaline dump into the bloodstream.

Anger can impact our ability to think and our communications; being angry clouds a person's mental processes. Expressed anger draws attention from the substance of the message. Hearers become more focused on the anger than the message.

When is anger okay and when is it a sin?

Chronic anger can impact relationships. Family members, coworkers, and friends feel they have to walk on eggshells around you when you are angry, which is much of the time. They fear how you will react when they speak honestly to you. Will you be verbally or physically aggressive?

The Bible tells us that human anger doesn't produce the righteousness that God wants (James 1:20); we are to stop being angry (Psalm 37:8). Below are seven ways anger moves from passion and

127

energy to agitation and boiling, perhaps from righteousness to damage.[19]

1) Your reason for being angry is selfishly motivated (James 1:20).

2) Your anger doesn't glorify God or defend his name (1 Corinthians 10:31).

3) Your anger continues so long that it gives the devil a foothold in your heart (Ephesians 4:26-27).

4) Your anger is volatile and brings emotional or physical harm to others (Psalm 37:8).

5) Your anger causes you to hold grudges against people with the intent of making them suffer (Ephesians 4:31).

6) Your anger makes you unable to forgive; you are consumed with revenge (Ephesians 4:32).

7) You hold on so tightly to anger that you feel depressed and irritable (Hebrews 12:15).

One of the angriest individuals I saw was in church. Loudly, she expressed her opinion of the new storage for choir robes. I couldn't relate. I ignored her, but we can't always ignore angry individuals, no matter what the setting. So how can we cope with or respond to individuals expressing anger, even more seriously, with individuals who seem to be chronically angry? This is a time when we can ask WWJD (what would Jesus do).

- Pray! Take the situation to God.
- Stay calm. Give the person space to regulate their own behavior. Let them know you are willing to

discuss the issue when they reassert control over themselves.

- Avoid making statements such as "Calm down, "it's not a big deal." Clearly, the situation is a big deal to the angry person.
- Stick to "I" statements, i.e., "I'm sad and scared when you yell at me."
- Remind yourself you aren't the cause of another person's anger. It's not your responsibility to fix it or them.
- Prioritize safety. Leave a dangerous situation.

Often, angry individuals seek assistance from pastors. Pastors aren't trained counselors. Pastors should refer angry persons for counseling, i.e., domestic violence or anger management support, or mental health counseling. Don't put your pastor into a situation that is outside his/her vocation. Worse yet, if the target of your anger is a spouse, you may be asking the pastor to take sides in a family dispute which is unfair to the pastor.

****

Habakkuk is a dialogue between the prophet and God. Habakkuk lived in Jerusalem prior to the Babylonian exile. In his short three-chapter book, Habakkuk complains to God and questions God's decisions. His book is a model for Christians to use when they complain to God. My default setting is complaining, so I resonated with and learned from Habakkuk.

In the first chapter, Habakkuk asks God why there is violence, injustice, strife, and conflict around him. Habakkuk sounds like he is watching the evening news and questioning what he sees. Instead, Habakkuk walked out his front door in Jerusalem in early 600 BCE and saw wickedness throughout the city.

Beginning in Habakkuk 1:5, God answers Habakkuk's first complaint about the amount of violence, injustice, etc. in Jerusalem, and what God is going to do about it. God tells Habakkuk that he plans to send the Babylonians to hold the Jerusalemites accountable for their behavior.

Habakkuk (1:12-17) is stunned by God's answer. He responds: surely not the Babylonians! They are more depraved and perverse than Jerusalemites. Why would God use such an ungodly hoard to punish a people more righteous than themselves?

Habakkuk wanted God's answer to be acceptable to him. Habakkuk wanted a king such as Josiah to clean up Jerusalem's streets and return Jerusalemites to God-worship. Instead, Jerusalem will get the Babylonians!

Today, godly people note that the world is a miserable place to live in. Earth is filled with sin, destruction, and calamity. Christians ask God, "Why do you let the wicked flourish and good people suffer? Where is your justice? Isn't justice supposed to be one of your attributes?" They may add: "Why are you taking so long to come back and establish your new Heaven and Earth?"

Similar to Habakkuk, Jesus-believers want God to give them their preferred answer and give it right now, rather than God's omniscient answer in God's time.

What do you do when God gives you an unwelcome answer to prayer?

Complaining to God about circumstances is okay with God. God knows Christians are sometimes bewildered by what's happening around them and to them. The omniscient God knows what we think before we tell him. He knows what we think even when we don't tell him directly. God wants us to pour out our emotions, i.e., pain, frustration, bewilderment, and anger, to him.

Sometimes complaining is evil and from Satan, but it isn't always evil or from Satan.[20] God wants us to tell him our troubles, even to complain to him. What God doesn't want and what is often from Satan is grumbling, as the rabble/Israelites in the desert (Numbers 11:4-9). When we grumble, we say that God isn't sufficiently good, loving, wise, or powerful. If God really had these characteristics, he would have acted differently.

There are right and wrong ways to complain to God. Ultimately, it comes down to the words that come out of our mouths and, perhaps, more importantly, the attitude of our hearts.[20] Although Habakkuk questioned God's way of doing things, he modeled acceptance of God's plans. Two verses acknowledges God sovereignty.

131

For the earth will be filled with the knowledge
of the glory of the Lord (Habakkuk 2:14).

Habakkuk said that eventually all of Earth will
see the glory of God and that God's ways are best.
Habakkuk's complaints are and will be nothing but
minor, insignificant details. Last evening, I sat on my
back deck and watched the wind blowing through the
trees and squirrels frolicking. God provided this
beautiful picture. In the future, all individuals on
Earth will see and know the glory of God. Earth isn't
going to be filled with the knowledge of the USA or
even a world-renowned politician or preacher. Earth
will be filled with the knowledge of God.

I will stand my watch… I will look to see
what he (God) will say…. to this complaint
(Habakkuk 2:1).

Isn't that what we are to do when we
complain to God? We are to watch and learn how
God will answer us.

These verses cited from Habakkuk mean that
God has the world under control. God doesn't need
our input, including our complaints, but God loves to
hear from us. I've come to believe that my repeated
complaints are designed to move my thoughts in line
with God's perfect plan for me. Are you there yet? If
not, pray and keep praying that God will get you
there. You may want to keep a prayer journal and
determine how the content of your prayers on a topic
changes over time.

There are three positive approaches we can take when bringing concerns (complaints) to God. First, resolve not to sin with your words (Psalm 17:3). That's hard, and few of us are able to reach that standard all the time, but keep trying. I think that God gives us credit for sincerely trying.

Second, approach God with an attitude of genuine inquiry versus an arrogant demand. At times, I blurt out impulsive words. That's why I believe that our hearts are as important, or more important, than our words when we talk to God. God knows our hearts and what we want and need even when our words are confusing and irrelevant (Romans 8:26).

Third, accepting God's plan versus insisting on our own plan. Remember Isaiah 55:8,9:

For my thoughts are not your thoughts, neither are your ways my ways, declares the LORD. As the heavens are higher than the earth, so are my ways higher than your ways and my thoughts than your thoughts.

The final chapter in Habakkuk is a prayer:

Though the fig tree does not bud and there are no grapes on the vines, though the olive crop fails and the fields produce no food, though there are no sheep in the pen and no cattle in the stalls yet I will rejoice in the LORD, I will be joyful in God my Savior (Habakkuk 3:17-18).

Habakkuk accepts that there will be famine in the land, the Babylonians will overrun Jerusalem, humans and livestock will die; nevertheless, Habakkuk determines that he will rejoice in God.

In the 21st century, Christians in westernized cultures could feel depressed when they look at the world around them. If they are—when they are—they can remember another of Habakkuk's insights, "But the Lord is in his holy temple; let all the earth be silent before him" (Habakkuk 2:20).

****

Eventually, the Babylonians overran Jerusalem. Many Judahites were exiled throughout the Babylonian Empire. Seventy-five years later, Zechariah was God's prophet in Judea after the Jews returned from their captivity. At that time, Judea was a tiny province in the Persian Empire. The Israelite kingdom no longer existed.

In the first year of his ministry, Zechariah received eight visions. The first vision was a parable. Zechariah saw a man on a horse among myrtle trees that grew in a ravine. The symbolism of Zechariah's first vision was tied to the myrtle tree, the ravine, and the status of returned Jews.

Previously, the symbol of the Israelite kingdom was the cedar of Lebanon, a giant, majestic tree. Now it is an understory tree, the myrtle. The myrtle tree only grew in the shadow of taller trees. In Zechariah's vision, the myrtle grew in a low point in the landscape. The tree could be damaged by cold, dry winds that blew through the ravine and cold air that settled in the base of the ravine. Similarly, Judea could be easily damaged, even destroyed, by enemies.

Like Jews newly returned to Judea, USA Christians and Christian churches in the 21st century experience upheaval and chaos. Individuals, inside and outside the body of Jesus, question the truth and relevance of Holy Scripture and God's statutes. As the vision of the man among the myrtle tree was a message of hope and encouragement to the postexile Jews, it's a message of hope to 21st-century Christians.

Given the Bible's predictions of end-times, is it okay to pray for peace on Earth?

The meaning of the word hope has changed from Bible times to its current usage in the USA society. Currently, when Americans use the word "hope," it encompasses an element of doubt. "I hope so" means a desire that may not materialize. Hope has become a wish. In contrast, in both Hebrew (*botah*[5]) and Greek (*elpis*[5]), hope means confidence, security, and assurance from God. Biblical hope isn't a feeling; it's a reality.

Notice the change in the definition of "hope" from Bible times to the 21st century? Ponder these three definitions of hope in common usage.

- The Bible definition is confident, assured belief.
- Webster's dictionary defines "hope" as a desire.
- 21st-century westernized society's definition of 'hope' includes the element of doubt and wishful thinking.

Wouldn't you feel more assured of God's presence if you followed the biblical definition of hope? Biblical hope expects something to happen.

In the 21st century, Christians shouldn't change the meaning of biblical "hope." For example, consider Psalm 42:12, "Why are you cast down, O my soul? Why so disturbed within me? Put your hope in God." Think about the verse if it were written, "Put your confidence and security in God." That's what the verse means.

Satan took a beautiful Bible word—hope—and eroded it in society and in our minds to the point where we don't trust God's words and aren't assured of the biblical promise of hope.

Hoping (putting our security) in God doesn't come naturally to sinners like us. We must preach 'hope' to ourselves, reminding ourselves that we can be assured of "hope" in Jesus. We can have a reservoir of God-belief (hope) to call upon when life goes sideways; an unwavering belief that God's word is true and that God is in us through our lowest moments. We can use "hope" to live a life of holiness in the worst circumstances.

Read slowly and commit to believing the words of this old hymn.

My Hope is Built On Nothing Less[21]

My hope is built on nothing less
Than Jesus' blood and righteousness;
I dare not trust the sweetest frame,
But wholly lean on Jesus' name.

When darkness veils His lovely face,
I rest on His unchanging grace;
In ev'ry high and stormy gale
My anchor holds within the veil.

His oath, His covenant, His blood
Support me in the whelming floods;
When all around my soul gives way,
He then is all my hope and stay.

When He shall come with trumpet sound,
O may I then in Him be found,
Dressed in His righteousness alone,
Faultless to stand before the throne.

Promise that your hope is in God during highs and lows.

Delving Deeper

Elijah commanded Israelites to kill the approximately 400 Ba'al prophets. Did he invite Queen Jezebel's persecution on himself by this command? Was it okay for him to order all of these men killed?

Before reading this interpretation of the Poem of the Plowman, what meaning did you get from these verses in Isaiah? How can you assist others to delve into the root meaning of the poem?

According to the prophet Hosea and other Bible writers, idolatry (putting anything before God) is a sin. Idolatry is as bad as adultery. Why do most of us commit both sins? What are your idols? How can you remove them from your life?

Do you believe that women can be/should be prophetesses? Why or why not?

How did Jews' perception of themselves as a nation change from pre-exile to post-exile? How did they get to return to Judah from the Babylonian captivity?

Living in the 21st-century USA, what is the basis for your hope? How are you able to remain hopeful in today's materialistic society?

Chapter 7

HERE COMES THE SON

Written by George Harrison, "Here Comes the Sun"[22] anticipates a better day. As the Son takes over, sadness and pressures melt away, optimism and anticipation appear. This metaphor is ideal for demonstrating the effect of Jesus' coming to Earth as God's Son.

There's a difference between saying you are a Christian and believing that Jesus is God and the only path to salvation and eternal life. When you read this chapter, you read a sample of Jesus' teachings, parables, and miracles, and see his life in action. Each section attests to Jesus as God. Christians believe that God has three aspects: Father, Son, and Holy Spirit.

Do you believe that Jesus is God?

Was Jesus God? Or was Jesus merely a good man, moral teacher, religious leader, or prophet? For 2000 years, humankind has debated that question. Currently, almost half (44 percent) of evangelical Christians say that Jesus was merely a great teacher, but not God.[23] They name themselves Christians, but reject Jesus' testimony that he was the Son of God and therefore God.

Below are five categories of evidence that support Jesus as God.[23] How much of this evidence an individual believes is an internal decision.

1) Prophecy: Jesus fulfilled 300 Old Testament prophecies about the Messiah.

2) Self-testimony: Jesus said he was the Son of God and God himself (Mark 14:61-63).

3) Behavior of apostles and disciples: Before Jesus' death, disciples and apostles were tentative, unsure of what they believed. Afterward, they boldly preached Jesus' divinity and salvation through him.

4) Archeology: Archeological evidence points to the truth of places where Bible stories were set.

5) Jesus' birth and death changed the world: Christianity didn't exist before Jesus.

Are you going to accept the evidence outlined above, or are you going to discount all or portions of it? Acceptance is how you become a Christian, not by checking some box on a government or employment application form.

Jesus-believers must follow Jesus' teachings. That's where our work really starts as we try to be more like him. This process is called sanctification. To move forward in the sanctification process, we read the Bible, paying particular attention to Jesus' teachings in the Gospels. But reading isn't enough! Each of us has to ask: How does that episode apply to me? Then, apply it to his/herself.

****

Are you more important than a black bird? Then, why don't you act like it? That's the question that Jesus asked listeners in 1st-century Galilee and asks them in 21st-century USA.

This episode from the gospel of Matthew (Matthew 5:1-7:28) is part of "The Sermon on the Mountain." In the Sermon on the Mountain, Jesus explained what he expected from his followers. I am going to focus on Jesus' teaching on worry (Matthew 6:25-34). Below are some verses from the "Do Not Worry" section of Matthew chapter six.

> Therefore I tell you, do not worry about your life, what you will eat or drink; or about your body, what you will wear (Matthew 6:25).

> Look at the birds of the air; they do not sow or reap or store away in barns, and yet your heavenly Father feeds them. Are you not much more valuable than they? (Matthew 6:26).

So do not worry, saying, 'What shall we eat?' or 'What shall we drink?' or 'What shall we wear?' Your heavenly Father knows that you need them (Matthew 6:31). But seek first his kingdom and his righteousness, and all these things will be given to you as well (Matthew 6:33).

Therefore do not worry about tomorrow, for tomorrow will worry about itself. Each day has enough trouble of its own (Matthew 6:34).

Anxiety is an extreme uneasiness of mind, even a brooding fear, about something that may or may not come to pass. Worry is mental anxiety expressed in words and behaviors. My aunt was a worrier. We heard her anxieties, her concerns, her dour predictions. She lived a life of "what if." What if this happens? What if that happens?

Remember the old saying that we don't need to borrow trouble by speculating about what could happen? Or better yet, as Jesus put it: By worrying can anyone add a single hour to life (Matthew 6:27)?

Pastor John MacArthur[24] believes that worry is a sin. He projected that a majority of mental and physical illnesses are related to worry. Worry incapacitates individuals. They are too upset to accomplish anything positive in the situation and possibly in other avenues of life.

When you worry, you are saying you don't trust God to take care of you, you don't believe

Scripture and are mastered by circumstance rather than mastering circumstances.[24]

If worry is a sin, has dire physical and mental consequences, and shows distrust, even disbelief in God, then why do we—who self-identify as Jesus-followers—worry? Possible reasons are:[24]

- We copy and repeat parental behavior. We learned to worry from our parents.
- Worry gives us something to talk about. Sharing worries makes us the center of attention. We get an ego boost from others listening to us.
- Worry releases anxiety in us. We feel a physical and mental sense of relief, which is a positive reinforcement, so we do the same thing the next time we are anxious.

Think about other reasons you worry and add them to the list.

Why do you do something such as worry, which is unproductive?

My aunt, the previously mentioned worrier, was a born-again Christian. Christians worry. Faith is present even among negative behaviors, but why not eliminate negatives when possible? Below are some ways that you can short-circuit worry.

1) Be aware! When you find yourself anxious and worrying, stop immediately. You might want to say "God's got this" aloud several times.

Doing so can replace and negate worry by focusing on a positive.

2) Take the problem to God. Remember, God never promised you an easy life; quite the contrary. Nowhere in the Bible does God say that all problems disappear when you begin to follow Jesus.

3) Memorize Bible verses about worry that you can substitute for your worry. My go-to verses are Philippians 4:6-7.

> Do not be anxious about anything, but in every situation, by prayer and petition, with thanksgiving, present your requests to God. And the peace of God, which transcends all understanding, will guard your hearts and your minds in Christ Jesus.

4) Have a Christian accountability partner who helps you reduce, even stop, worrying. This accountability partner needs to be a mature Christian, so you don't use the individual for attention-getting or as a counselor. Remember, your accountability partner's primary role isn't to be a listener to every tiny aspect of your worry episode, but to move you to focus on God in the situation.

5) Some individuals are so immersed in worry that they have nothing else to think about. Paul suggested that Christians ponder what is true (many times worry isn't true), noble, lovely, right, and pure (Philippians 4:8). Thinking about these positive topics rather than worrying about a situation that may never occur or that you can't change.

6) Christians live in a different reality. Our new reality is Jesus in us, our ongoing deliverer. You

no longer have to worry about situations that earthly-minded individuals worry about.

****

Jesus taught truths about God, Heaven, and salvation through parables. A parable is a comparison in which an image borrowed from the visible world points to a truth in the spiritual world. In the parable of the 10 bridesmaids (Matthew 25:1-15), Jesus pointed to the return of the Son of God to Earth (Matthew chapter 24).

The 10 young bridesmaids waited at night to accompany the groom and bride from the bride's home to the groom's. Each bridesmaid had a lamp to light streets, but it was the contents of the lamp that counted.

The bride and groom were delayed in leaving the bride's home. The young bridesmaids fell asleep. When the couple left the home, five unprepared bridesmaids didn't have sufficient oil in their lamp to fuel it when they walked through the streets. They had to leave the wedding party to purchase additional oil.

In the meantime, the groom, bride, and five prepared bridesmaids entered the groom's home for the marriage festival. Later, the five unprepared bridesmaids arrived at the groom's home. They were denied entry because they were late arriving.

In this parable, the groom is Jesus, and the groom's home is Heaven. The virgins were humans. Some humans are wise. They have accepted Jesus as their Savior. They are filled with the Holy Spirit. They are ready to enter Heaven.

Some humans aren't wise. They may know about Jesus, but don't know him as their Savior. The Holy Spirit doesn't live in them; consequently, they aren't prepared to accompany Jesus into Heaven.

"Be Prepared" is the motto of the Boy Scouts of America.[2] Scouts believe they should be prepared for life and to live happily and without regret, knowing that they have done their best.

"Be prepared" should be the goal of every Christian—ready to help other believers, ready to assist and witness to non-believers, ready for Jesus' return. Ideally, preparation to enter Heaven is a two-step process. We can stop after step one, but why would we want to? It would be like buying tickets to a concert but not being prepared to attend.

Step one in preparation for Heaven is accepting Jesus as our Savior. That's named "justification." From God's perspective, we became just as if we never sinned. We can stop after step one; the groom will open Heaven's door and invite us in. But why deprive ourselves of living a life centered on Jesus?

Let's go to Step 2. Like Boy Scouts are productive citizens and give happiness to others, so Jesus-followers can embody Jesus in situations they find themselves in on Earth.

Imagine yourself as a bridesmaid's lamp emitting happiness into your world.

Think about your lamp (you)! Are you filled with the Holy Spirit at your workplace? You are kind to others rather than in constant competition with them, patient with their idiosyncrasies, and rejoice in their accomplishments? With this attitude, you are seen as highly valued.

Now take your imagination a step further. What if you wanted to be productive and give happiness to others at church and in your family? You wouldn't insist on having your own way. Likely, you wouldn't care where the choir robes were stored.

How do we become prepared? How do we live in readiness for Jesus' second coming? How do you make sure your oil doesn't run out as you wait for the second coming of Jesus? Some suggestions are:

1) Communicate and stay connected with God. We do this by praying. In prayer, we express our love and gratitude to God. Jesus told followers to pray that they don't fall into temptation (Matthew 26:41).

2) Study the Bible. Study is more than a systematic read through the Bible, albeit a great idea. Synonyms of study are learn, train, and investigate. Take a deep dive into God's instruction book for your life.

3) Give happiness to others.[25] What a great idea! We give happiness to others by serving them. The bridesmaids served the groom by lighting his way through dark streets.

4) Share life/fellowship with other believers. Fellowship helps us see we aren't alone in this

journey through life. Also, we enrich the lives of others.

Living in readiness for the second coming of Jesus isn't a burden or fear. It's the anticipation of being invited to go through the bridegroom's door. At the same time, we have to be prepared.

****

Jesus had an active prayer life. Do you? In the Bible, Jesus is recorded as praying 30 plus times. He prayed around key events in his life, for example, being baptized, starting his ministry, and before being put on trial, tortured, and crucified. Jesus prayed thanksgiving before meals, i.e., feeding the 5000 and before the Last Supper. Jesus prayed blessings on children. When they asked, Jesus taught his disciples a prayer. At times, Jesus went off by himself to pray. At other times, Jesus prayed with others around him.

Just as Jesus made prayer a central part of his life. Jesus instructs us, his followers, to make prayer a central part of our lives. Jesus told us to not only pray for our families, nation, and ourselves but to pray for our enemies (Matthew 5:24). No, we aren't to pray that our enemies' lives will be disastrous but for their well-being. That is a tough command to follow. When was the last time you asked God to bless that person who really annoys you or has hurt you?

Prayer isn't meant to be one-sided—gimme, gimme, gimme—from you to God. Prayer is talking with God, a two-way communication in which both parties talk. God is always available to hear our prayers, whether we send a quick text message to him or spend more time with him.

Can you imagine never talking to your spouse, friends, or parents, i.e., ignoring them? Not telling them you are hungry, hurt, lonely? Not telling them you love them and are thankful for all they have done for you? They love you; they want you to tell them what you need. Even more than your parents/spouse/friends want to talk with you, so does God.

Jesus' disciples wanted to know how to pray, and so do 21st-century Christians. Below is the prayer that Jesus gave disciples. In the 21st century, we name it "The Lord's Prayer."

> Our Father who art in heaven, hallowed be thy name. Thy kingdom come, thy will be done, on earth as it is in heaven. Give us this day our daily bread. And forgive us our trespasses as we forgive those who trespass against us. And, lead us not into temptation, but deliver us from evil, for thine is the kingdom and the glory forever. Amen

Various Bible teachers give formulas and models for prayer. They include the ACTS acronym (Adoration, Confession, Thanksgiving and Supplication); using a daily psalm to focus thoughts; reading the daily liturgy and prayers from *The Book of Common Prayer*; integrating prayer in all activities of life, such as suggested by Brother Lawrence;[2] journaling; singing; and praying with

149

hands lifted. There's no one correct method for prayer. At different times in our lives, we use different methods. That is totally okay.

Many pastors and Bible teachers advocate that Jesus-believers have a set time and a set place for daily prayer. That suggestion has value. It makes time and location a habitual part of our lives. My husband studies the Bible and prays every morning. He goes to his "man cave" and closes the door. A friend has a special chair. Another sits outside on her deck where she can see trees, birds, and flowers.

These locations for prayer are good, but so is the commode, jogging, driving your car, sitting at the table, and in church. We can communicate with God anywhere. God isn't like our parents or spouse, where we tell or ask them something only when we are in proximity to them or via electronic media.

When you pray, no matter what the method or place, you knock on Heaven's door. There's no need to demand God open the door or threaten that you won't follow him if he doesn't answer your prayer. You don't need to begin your prayer by reminding God how holy you are (Luke 18:9-14).

If God knows my needs, why do I have to pray?

Many churches and individuals pose the question, should we assume God knows and will automatically meet our needs, or should we pray about them? My personal opinion is that God knows our every need; however, we should pursue God. Ask

God for what you believe you need. Be sure to include "your will be done."

A fellow Christian believes that we should only ask God for something once. According to her, God hears us the first time. We don't need to repeat the same prayer to God. Her rationale is completely true; God always hears us the first time and remembers. On the other hand, Jesus told a parable of the widow before the judge (Luke 18:1-8). Jesus praised the widow for asking for justice multiple times. Likewise, for Christians in the 21st century, it's okay to be persistent in prayers to Father God.

Persistence in prayers—repeatedly talking with God about the same topic—gives space for God to change our minds so our perspective becomes more in line with God's. Doesn't that turn the rationale for your prayer life upside down? You want God to change your mind rather than you influencing God's mind!

Sooner or later, most of us who pray feel like we aren't connecting with God. Individuals have named this time in a Christian's life as a "dry season," "trough period," and the "dark night of the soul." When these times occur, you keep knocking on Heaven's door, but you don't feel God hears you. When Saint Mother Teresa of Calcutta[26] experienced a dry season in her prayer life, she wrote:

> God, please forgive me, when I try to raise my thoughts to heaven, there is such convicting emptiness that those very thoughts return like sharp knives and hurt my very soul. I am told God loves me, and yet the reality of darkness and coldness and

emptiness is so great that nothing touches my soul. Did I make a mistake in surrendering blindly to the call of the Sacred heart?

Don't stop knocking on Heaven's door even if it feels like no one is home. God is always home and ready to open the door. You are saved by God's grace alone, not by your prayers.

****

The significant Bible episode was between Jesus and a woman caught in adultery. This episode is controversial (John 8:1-11). In some Bible translations, this episode isn't there. Yet, the episode has implications for Christians who want to level up their walk with Jesus.

The setting was the Temple courtyard in Jerusalem. A group of men, of all ages, brought a woman caught in adultery to Jesus and asked Jesus what punishment the woman should receive. Most likely, she was a married woman who was having sexual intercourse with a man who wasn't her husband. The men forced the woman to stand in front of Jesus. The group reminded Jesus that Mosaic Law required that the woman be stoned to death. Then, the men asked Jesus what to do with her. Talk about a set-up for Jesus—this was it.

The men were judgmental. Their judgment showed condemnation of the woman. Christians have a reputation for being judgmental. That reputation alienates Christians from each other and Christians from non-Christians. Some individuals back away from Christians, thinking that Christians judge them. They don't want a "judgy" friend.

Jesus said that God is going to judge us using our standards of judgment (Matthew 7:1-6). How we condemn others will be God's standard for condemning us.

Alienation from God occurs when we judge others, maybe even when we are judging ourselves.

Jesus' message was straightforward (Luke 6:37-44). Don't judge, and you won't be judged. Don't condemn, and you won't be condemned. Forgive, and you will be forgiven. Don't attempt to take a speck of sawdust out of your brother's (or sister's) eye while you have a plank in your own eye.

Our judgments are biased. Writing in *Psychology Today*, Hiliary Handel[27] noted that we judge others through the lens of our own points of view. Her thoughts included:

- Personal emotions (anxiety, self-doubt, shame, and guilt) fuel our judgments of others.
- Being aware of personal emotions that underlie judgments of others helps us be more compassionate and less judgmental. We don't know the other person's heart or the motivations for their actions.
- Judgmental thoughts protect us. Individuals we encounter act differently than we act. Our actions can't be wrong, so their actions have to be wrong.

153

Ponder the verse "Every way of man is right in his own eyes" (Proverbs 21:2 NKJV).

When you think about being judgmental, consider how to change your attitude so that more individuals want to interact with you. Start with Jesus' directive to love others. Loving others is work. Becoming a nonjudgmental person takes prayer and practice. Below are four ways we can become more open-minded.[28]

1) Begin by developing self-awareness. Monitor your thoughts. Catch yourself making judgments. Note what triggers both positive and negative judgments. Making a judgment is an opportunity for introspection.

2) Reshape/revise/rewrite your judgmental thoughts (even if they are about yourself) using understanding and compassion. Journaling is a great way to note and replace judgmental thoughts.

3) Accept others. No, you don't have to be everyone's BFF, but don't let negative thoughts about them fester in your mind.

4) Expand your social circle to include individuals unlike you, i.e., the poor, individuals of another religion, and a person who has a different sexual orientation. Learn their unique challenges, even individuals you don't agree with. Practice compassion. Understanding can replace judgment.

****

Through miracles, Jesus showed his love and compassion for humans that God created. Jesus performed as many as 37 miracles in the Gospels. Most were healings, but he fed thousands of individuals and walked on water. At least three times, Jesus brought a dead person back to life.

Perhaps the best-known story of Jesus raising a dead person is the resurrection of Lazarus, dead for four days. This event was heart-rending for Jesus. Both of Lazarus' sisters, who Jesus loved, claimed that if Jesus had been there, Lazarus wouldn't have died (John 11:21).

Dictionaries, particularly Bible dictionaries, define miracles as events, signs, wonders, or experiences that demonstrate God's greatness and power. A miracle goes beyond typical human expectations that occur in the world. Miracles defy the laws of nature. They couldn't have occurred without supernatural intervention.

Each miracle Jesus performed in the Gospels had a purpose. Many met a serious human need or confirmed Jesus' identity and/or authority. Jesus bringing Lazarus back to life showed his authority over death.

From Jesus' years on Earth to around 1700 CE, when the Enlightenment Era (time of scientific reasoning) began, Jesus' miracles weren't questioned. With the Enlightenment, scholars began to search for alternative explanations for miracles. For example, they postulated that the crippled man that Jesus healed was in collusion with Jesus. In reality, he was always able to walk. Jesus' miracle of feeding 5000 occurred because people shared the lunches they brought with them. Seeing the resurrected Jesus was wishful thinking or mass delusion/hysteria.

Most of us have watched televangelists perform miraculous healings. We attended church services where we saw or heard about miraculous events. The questions are, "Are these true, supernatural events? Should we expect to see miracles today?" Many of us don't know when an event is a miracle or a deceitful happening. We want intimate knowledge of the situation before we conclude that a miracle occurs.

Many 21st-century Christians believe miracles occur today. Saturday morning, I was with five Christian women having coffee. All said they believed in miracles and experienced a miracle in their lives. One was healing for her husband. One occurred when she was in a car accident and was preserved safely. A nurse said that she saw babies that should have died go home fully normal. One friend said that her Christian women friends are a miracle from God.

When I lived in El Paso, a city across the river from Juarez, Mexico, a church took Thanksgiving dinner to residents of the Juarez dump. Church members believed they had more than enough food for all the dump residents who would come to eat. Yet, people kept coming and coming. Food started to get low. There were still long lines of hungry individuals. Food servers were getting nervous. Church members prayed that God would provide sufficient food for all people. God answered the prayers. All Jaurez dump residents received a

Thanksgiving meal. How do miracles apply in our walk with Jesus in the 21st century?

The greatest miracle that ever occurred was Christ coming to earth and living and dying for humanity.

Does believing in miracles enhance our ability to be more effective Christians? In a podcast, the noted clergyman John Piper[29] offered observations on miracles:

1) Jesus' miracles weren't to show that his kingdom was completed.

2) All Bible saints didn't perform miracles. Don't be depressed if you don't walk on water or accomplish a miraculous healing.

3) Probably, more miracles occur today than you realize, i.e., healings. On the other hand, we live in a time when suffering is normal. God won't remove all suffering. We need to lean on Jesus to support us during suffering.

4) When we repent, it isn't and shouldn't be on the basis of miracles that were recorded in the Bible or even that we've seen.

Piper[29] averred that the Christian looks forward with hope to eternal life with Jesus. Willingly, we suffer, love people, and call them to faith in Jesus. In our lives, miracles are nice and valued when they occur but aren't vital to belief in God.

Delving Deeper

What does it say about God that he would send his Son to Earth so that you can know him? What does it say about God's Son that he willingly came to Earth? Would you want to live to Earth in first century Palestine, i.e., no commodes, soft toilet paper, or warm showers? Think about having to bathe in the dirty Jordan River.

If you haven't read the Sermon on the Mountain (Matthew chapters 5-7) lately, read it. Identify the top three instructions you receive from these chapters. How will each change your life?

When you ponder Jesus' life, what's the most attractive thing about his character? Do you want to be like him? List life changes you are willing to make to be more like Jesus. List changes you aren't willing to make in your life.

Read the Lord's Prayer. Rewrite it to make it relevant to your life in the 21st century. Then, claim it by saying it daily. Don't neglect to do this exercise. It will deepen your walk with Jesus.

Do you question the occurrence of miracles? If you saw a miracle, would you more likely to believe in God? Alternatively, would you look for other "rational" explanations for what you saw?

Chapter 8

I SEE CLEARLY NOW

The New Testament church is the focus of Chapter 8, I See Clearly Now. The chapter title comes from a 1972 song, "I Can See Clearly."[30] It's about the hope and courage of people who have experienced adversity in their lives but have overcome it. The song is an ideal descriptor for the early Christian church.

God sent the Holy Spirit to live in and help Jesus-believers in the newly formed Christian community. Christians only see clearly when they look through the lens of Jesus. There is no greater influence on the church than the Holy Spirit. In the early church community, human influencers were primarily Peter, Paul, and James, the brother of Jesus.

Many of us understand God; we know the Old Testament and all God did there. We understand God's son, Jesus. He lived and died for us. Through believing in Jesus as Savior, we have eternal life. The Holy Spirit is harder to understand.

Often Christians ask where the Holy Spirit originated? The answer is that the Holy Spirit is God. The Holy Spirit is a part of the Trinity that includes God the Father, God the Son (Jesus Christ), and God the Holy Spirit. Where God is, the Holy Spirit is.

In four short verses, this Acts' episode described the Holy Spirit coming to indwell Jesus-followers. This event is named Pentecost because it occurred 50 days after Jesus' resurrection.

> When the day of Pentecost came, they were all together in one place. Suddenly a sound like the blowing of a violent wind came from heaven and filled the whole house where they were sitting. They saw what seemed to be tongues of fire that separated and came to rest on each of them. All of them were filled with the Holy Spirit and began to speak in other tongues as the Spirit enabled them (Acts 2:1-4).

The Holy Spirit enters individuals when they repent and ask Jesus to come into their lives. That's it! That's all it takes—sincerely asking Jesus to come into our life. The Holy Spirit is happy to do so.

In the 21st century, Christians want to live with God at the center of their lives. Sometimes, they can live that life spot on. Just as often, they get it wrong. The good news is that regardless of whether we get life right or wrong, the Holy Spirit remains in us. The Holy Spirit will be in us when Earth, as we know it, ends.

Perhaps one reason the Holy Spirit is confusing to Christians and non-Christians alike is that at one time we referred to him as the Holy Ghost. The word "ghost" conjures notions of the occult or eerie apparitions, which are far from the truth of the Holy Spirit. The Holy Spirit is the Christian's Helper and Advocate (John 14:16; John 14:26). Christians don't have to live life on their own. They can contact the Holy Spirit through prayer for small and big problems.

Most Christians don't turn to the Holy Spirit for help until they're desperate. We've tried multiple other strategies to solve a problem. Yet, as Christians, we can tap into the Holy Spirit's power anytime we need him. We don't have to be desperate.

Below are four ways the Holy Spirit helps Jesus-followers:

1) The Holy Spirit empowers us to be witnesses for Jesus. In Acts (1:8), Jesus told disciples that with the Holy Spirit's power, they could effectively witness for him throughout the world. Throughout the world, includes anywhere we are at any time, i.e., home, coffee shop, workplace, or church. Jesus' words imply that we shouldn't set aside specific times to be God's witnesses. Rather, we should be his witnesses at all times.

2) The Holy Spirit helps us to worship God (John 4:23-24). Whether we pray, reverently read the Bible, listen to praise music, etc., we worship God.

God approves multiple methods of worship.

3) The Holy Spirit allows us to bear fruit (Galatians 5:22-23). Bear fruit means that through the Holy Spirit, we can:

- Love God and love others.
- Take joy in our relationship with God and with each other.
- Feel peace and contentment.
- Have patience versus impatience with other individuals and with life events.
- Radiate kindness, goodness, and gentleness to others
- Remain faithful to God and to promises we made to individuals in our life, i.e., parents, spouses, and children.
- Control ourselves, particularly emotions and desires, in difficult situations.

4) The Holy Spirit gives gifts to the Church as a whole and to members of the Church (1 Corinthians 12:7-11). A spiritual gift is a special ability given to an individual by the Holy Spirit. The biggest and best gift that the Holy Spirit gives to the Church is the gift of himself. Every Christian has at least one spiritual gift (1 Corinthians 12:7). The most extensive list of gifts given to the church is identified in Corinthians.

Now to each one the manifestation of the Spirit is given for the common good. To one there is given through the Spirit a message of wisdom, to another a message of knowledge by means of the same Spirit, to another faith by the same Spirit, to another gifts of healing by that one Spirit, to another miraculous powers, to another prophecy, to another distinguishing between spirits, to another speaking in different kinds of tongues, and to still another the interpretation of tongues (1 Corinthians 12:7-11).

Once we know what the Holy Spirit is and what the Holy Spirit does, our next question is, "How can we tap into him to live a Spirit-filled life? The first step is to ask God for increased knowledge of the Spirit. That is a prayer God delights to answer.

Several decades ago, I sat alone in my living room reading my Bible. I came to a passage about the Holy Spirit. I stopped reading and said something to the effect, "I don't really understand you, Holy Spirit. Nor do I understand what you are supposed to do in my life. Will you please help me to know you better?" Since then, the Holy Spirit has become my "go-to" part of the Trinity. I take special joy in the Holy Spirit, knowing he is in me and helping me.

To focus your Holy Spirit study, do an internet search to locate Bible verses about the Holy Spirit. It matters little which Bible version you use. Read these verses. Pray to understand them. As you internalize these verses, God will increase your insight into the Holy Spirit's role in your life to include conviction of sins.

The Holy Spirit is in each of us to help us. Are you accepting the Spirit's help?

****

The book of Acts is just that—acts of believers in the newly formed Church. The description of the Holy Spirit entering believers at Pentecost is a message of "Happy Birthday." Pentecost Sunday is the birthday of the Christian Church. Every Sunday (at a minimum), Christians come together and have a birthday party.

The Christian community is named the universal Church. The Church is the collective life of individuals who have repented of sins and asked Jesus to live in them. When the universal Church is referenced, often the "c" in church is capitalized. The Church is part of God's eternal purpose (Ephesians 3:10-11).

In addition to the universal Church, there are local churches. Local churches are usually buildings where individuals come together to worship God; however, some individuals worship together in a home, a coffee shop, or park. Jesus said that where 2-3 gather in his name, he will be there (Matthew 18:20).

In New Testament times, when a church was identified, i.e., church in Corinth, Ephesus, etc., generally, a local church was meant. Church members met together because they held a similar belief in Jesus as Savior. They wanted to worship Jesus with individuals who believed like they believed. They wanted the Spirit's help and support of fellow Christians as they encountered challenges in their lives. In the 21st century, Jesus believers want the same things.

The purposes of local churches and the universal Church are the same. Below are six purposes:

1) Evangelize. Take Jesus' message of salvation to the entire world, including next-door neighbors and colleagues at work.

2) Teach. Declare instructions, guidance, and warnings from God, while having no division in the church body.

3) Baptize believers. When Jesus-followers are baptized, this is a sign to the world where their allegiance lies.

4) Contend (struggle) for the faith. Stir up one another to express love and good works. Encourage one another and at times rebuke one another.

5) Fellowship together to include sharing the Eucharist (Communion).

6) Support church ministers and ministries with voluntary generosity (1 Corinthians 9:13-14).

Often, the human body is used as a metaphor for the Church, both universal and local. God is the head of the body (1 Corinthians 12:12-31; Colossians 1:9-10). The great missionary of the early Church, Paul, said that no individual body part can succeed alone. Each part is needed to make a perfect body. Likewise, in the 21st-century church, each member is needed for a healthy body. You can't opt out of all church activities. You are needed.

Different members of the universal Church and local churches have different roles, i.e., apostles, prophets, evangelist, pastors, teachers, and elders (Ephesians 4:11; 1 Timothy 5:17). The reason for varied roles was and is to equip the church for works of service a) so the entire body would be built up, b) to promote unity in faith and knowledge, and c) assist members to mature in the faith (Ephesians 4:12-13).

Rarely can an individual by him/herself mature their walk with Jesus. They need a group, a tribe, in today's vocabulary. Finding the right church isn't easy. Recently, my husband and I decided to change churches. We visited multiple churches until we found the one we now attend. My girlfriends visited churches for two years before they found the right one.

When you look for a church, your first question should be whether or not the church's doctrine and teachings adhere to Jesus' teachings. If they don't, remove the church from your consideration list. Almost all local churches publish statements of beliefs on their church website.

Church doctrine is an important first step in selecting a church, but so are opinions and teachings at the local church level. Sometimes, a local church decides to stop following a denomination's doctrinal element or adds a belief statement. A personal example occurred in the church we attended for 10 years. The pastor decided to no longer adhere to one of the denomination's core (doctrinal) values. As his ideas changed, so did what he preached and practiced. For us, the change was so important that we changed churches.

Because 10 years ago you evaluated consistency between a church's doctrine and actions and those of the New Testament, it doesn't mean you can forgo future evaluations. The time frame for evaluating church doctrine and the application of doctrine in the local church is at least every five years.

After locating a Bible-based church, look for Bible studies to take and groups to join. Make friends. It's almost impossible to be a lone-ranger Christian. Most churches have small groups with a maximum of 7-12 church members. Your small group becomes your family in the church tribe. These are the individuals that you open yourself to. You study the Word together and get together for holidays. Ideally, some of these people will be your BFFs. They hold the same spiritual and moral-ethical values as you.

The early Christian church emphasized the importance of each believer serving others. They showed God's love through acts of kindness, generosity, and compassion. In the 21st-century church, the "80/20 syndrome" is present in some churches. This syndrome alludes to 80% of church work is done by 20% of individuals. In reality, individual members of the body of Jesus don't have the option of non-participation while being obedient to God.

How likely did the 80/20 syndrome operate in 1st-century churches?

****

In the initial years of the Christian church, believers shared property and possessions. The church had no starving individuals because of the generosity of wealthy members; however, not everything in the 1st-century church was perfect, just like not everything is perfect in the 21st-century church. A church couple, Ananias and Sapphira, sold a piece of land (Acts 5:1-11). They told Peter and church leaders that they were giving the church the entire selling price of the land. In actuality, they gave the Jerusalem church a portion of the selling price while keeping the remainder for themselves.

Peter confronted Ananias with his duplicity, accusing him of lying to the church and to God/Holy Spirit. In fear, Ananias fell down dead. Later, Sapphira entered the church group. She confirmed that the land's selling price was the amount Ananias told Peter. Peter accused Sapphira of lying to the Holy Spirit. She too fell dead. The episode demonstrated that the Holy Spirit in the new Church was greater than Satan's machinations.

Ananias and Sapphira lied. The Bible presented a negative perspective on lying 2000-3000 years ago. In the interim between then and the 21st century, God didn't change his mind about telling lies. Telling the truth is as important today as millennia ago. Below are some God-perspectives on lying:

- Lying lips are an abomination to the Lord (Proverbs 12:22).
- Do not be arrogant and lie against the truth (James 3:14).
- He who tells lies will perish (Proverbs 19:9).
- Laying aside falsehood, speak truth to each one of you with his neighbor, for we are members of one another (Ephesians 4:25).

Sin was introduced into God's pristine creation in the Garden of Eden through a lie. Sin was introduced to the early Christian church through a lie. Satan hasn't change his tactics. Satan lies or works on individuals to lie.

Despite God's prohibition against lying and the dire consequences for lying, about 1/3 of participants in a recent research study admitted lying 3-7 times per week.[31] The majority said they lied 2-3 times each week. Participants gave four main reasons for lying:

1) For altruistic (64%) reasons, to include telling a lie to make others feel better or protect others from harm. Do you ever tell your pastor, "That was a great sermon," when it was mediocre at best?

2) To keep personal information secret. You don't want your child's teacher to know that your child gets care from a government-funded clinic, so you talk about his/her private physician.

3) To avoid being judged. You tell colleagues in the workplace you graduated from a private university when you attended a community college.

You don't want them to believe you were poorly educated.

4) To impress others and to present yourself in a positive light. Most likely this is the reason Ananias and Sapphira colluded about the selling price of their field. They wanted to be admired by others in the budding church community. Perhaps, beneath their desire for admiration was denial of negative aspects in themselves, i.e., greed, not trusting God, feeling inadequate.

God's and Society's perspectives on lying disagree.

21st-century psychologists[31] argued that if individuals lie for altruistic reasons (i.e., to protect others from harm), the lies aren't always immoral, malicious, or unethical. In other words, if the liar deceives for a good reason, the lie is okay.

These psychologists assert that altruistic lies are part of the glue that binds families, social groups, workplaces, and churches together. Often, altruistic individuals put others' interests ahead of their own interests.

Altruistic lies may sound acceptable, even admirable, in a religious community; however, we need to delve deeper. The first question to ask when you consider lying is "What would Jesus do in a similar situation?" Jesus wouldn't lie!

The second question is what happens to our witness for Jesus if the truth comes out? At a minimum, we are embarrassed. Our Christian witness is compromised. Individuals assume that if you tell a "little, white" lie, you will have no problem telling a "big, black" lie.

****

The conversion of Saul on the Damascus Road was the next salient episode in the new Church. Saul (Paul) was the greatest Christian missionary of the first century, but he didn't start out that way. Initially, Paul, a dedicated Jew, persecuted followers of The Way, as Jesus-followers were named at that time.

Saul traveled, most likely walked, from Jerusalem to Damascus. In Damascus, he planned to take men and women who belonged to the Way as prisoners (Acts 9:2). On the road to Damascus, Saul saw a brilliant light from Heaven. A voice identified himself as Jesus and asked Saul the reason Saul persecuted him. If Saul gave an answer to the question, the Acts episode didn't record it. From the encounter, Saul was blinded and remained blind for three days.

Then, a Jesus disciple, Ananias, visited Saul and restored his sight. Saying Ananias didn't want to go to Saul is an understatement (Acts 9:13-14); yet Ananias did as the Lord directed. After Ananias placed his hands on his eyes, Saul's sight was restored. Saul was baptized. Saul's name was changed to Paul. Paul became a missionary, primarily to Gentiles.

Before Paul met Jesus on the Damascus road, he was spiritually blind—he was blind to the reality that Jesus was God. Pastor John Brennan[32] of

Bethlehem Church in Hampden, Massachusetts wrote that Christians have scales on their eyes that prohibit spiritual growth, including growing into a deeper relationship with the Savior. He added that from time to time we need to change our perspective, look at things differently, so scales fall off our eyes.

Brennan gave five suggestions to remove scales from our eyes, that is, change our perspective:

1) Attend church. In the 21st century, Americans don't appreciate the importance of consistent church attendance. Have you ever considered that your spotty attendance influences the attendance of others? When we don't attend church regularly, we say that we don't see the value of making a weekly commitment. Early Jesus-believers didn't have that perspective. Instead, they believed, "Do not give up meeting together" (Hebrews 10:25).

2) Involve yourself in ministry. Things get done in a church through the efforts of congregates. If we aren't willing to minister (serve, participate), something good is lost from your church. When your children notice—and they do notice—that their parents don't serve, they conclude serving others isn't important.

3) Read your Bible. Knowing the purpose for our lives comes through reading the Bible. We can never show our purpose if we don't know what it is.

What is the purpose of your life?

4) Get Christian education. Every church has a Christian education committee that provides

teaching for congregates. Also, many churches believe they need to send missionaries into the world to provide education to non-Christians and young Christians (Matthew 28:19-20).

What percent of your church's members attend Christian education offerings, something as easy as Sunday school? You can't put into practice what you don't know. If you don't know what Jesus taught, you can't practice it. Nor can you teach others.

5) Live daily for God's glory. We are so immersed in our own glory that it's hard to find time and energy to give God glory. (Please reread that sentence because it is so true.) We don't point people to God because we want them to focus on us. Paul wrote to the Christians at Corinth, " So whether you eat or drink or whatever you do, do it all for the glory of God" (1 Corinthians 10:31). If we choose to do so, we can give glory to God in our relationships, cheering for a sports team, or even participating in Christian education.

Remember the song "Amazing Grace" by John Newton:[33]

Amazing grace! how sweet the sound,
That saved a wretch like me!
I once was lost, but now am found.
Was blind, but now I see.

Each of us has had spiritual blindness at one time or another. We can't cure our own spiritual blindness; only Jesus can.

****

In the 21ˢᵗ century, the vast majority of Christians are non-Jewish; however, early in Christian Church history, Jesus-followers were Jews. Those of us who are Gentiles rejoice in the following New Testament episode between Peter and Cornelius that enfolds us into the Christian church.

Cornelius was a centurion in the Roman military. Although not a Jew, he worshiped God. An angel visited Cornelius and told him to send for Peter. Meanwhile, Peter had a vision of a large sheet containing all kinds of creatures, i.e., animals, birds, and reptiles, lowered from Heaven. A voice instructed Peter to kill and eat them. Peter refused, naming the creatures impure and unclean. The voice told Peter, "Do not call anything impure that God has made clean" (Acts 10:14). That verse is the key to the entire Peter-Cornelius episode.

When Cornelius' envoy arrived at Peter's lodging, they persuaded Peter to accompany them to Cornelius' home in Caesarea. There, Peter shared with Cornelius, his family, and friends the story of Jesus' life, death, and resurrection. As Peter spoke, the Holy Spirit came upon all who heard the message. Hearers spoke in tongues.

Peter concluded that these Gentiles should be baptized in the name of Jesus Christ. Later, the Jerusalem Council approved Peter's actions, concluding "even to the Gentile God has granted repentance that leads to life" (Acts 11:18).

The Bible episode of Peter and Cornelius is about equality and equity. Christian equality asserts that all individuals are equal in Jesus' sight. Equity is impartiality. God expects Christians to exhibit both.

> *When you think "equity" think impartiality.*

In 21st century churches, equality for all believers is problematic. Separation occurs on the basis of race, gender, sexual preference, etc. Today in the USA, inequality/inequity isn't a Jew-Gentile separation but remains a racial one. In the 1963 Martin Luther King said "11 o'clock in Sunday morning is one of the most segregated hours, if not the most segregated hour, in Christian America."[34]

Not much has changed in the 60 plus years since King's famous statement. Inequality/inequity remains in almost all church settings. Notice my use of the small "c" in church, that's because inequality/inequity doesn't come from the Holy Spirit, the source of the universal Church. God calls all believers without regard to class, gender, or race to roles and ministries inside and outside the Church.

Below are some Bible verses about equality and equity. They guide our reality as we try to treat people impartially. As you read them, contemplate how serious the Bible is about equity among humankind.

- Is God the God of the Jews only? Is he not the God of the Gentiles also (Ecclesiastes 3:19)?
- There is neither Jew nor Greek, there is neither slave nor free man, there is neither male nor

female; for all are one in Christ Jesus (1
Corinthians 12:25)
- There is no partiality with God (Ephesians 6:9).
- For there is no distinction; for all have sinned
  (Romans 2:11).
- If you show partiality, you are committing sin (1
  Timothy 5:21).

Equality/equity should matter to Christians.
It's a critical truth in the Christian faith. How can
21st-century Christians get on board with God's plan
for equity? We are surrounded by a cacophony of
voices that demand we promote equity this way or
that way. What is the best way?

Derick Smith[35] identified habits that
Christians should learn if they want to promote
equality and equity in the church.

1) Drop the labels. We need to stop
identifying churches as a White church, Black
church, Asian church, etc. Referring to a church by
its ethnicity, can limit who attends. For example, a
White individual may be reluctant to attend an
"Asian church".

2) Stop being so sensitive. Smith[35] noted that
if we are easily offended, possibly we think too
highly of ourselves.

3) Choose relationships over comfort. I grew
up in a rural setting surrounded by people who
looked like me. When I entered the Army, I met
individuals of different ethnicities. The Army
promoted racial and gender equality. I built
relationships with individuals of all races and

176

religions. It wasn't hard. We were more alike than different.

4) Diversify your church. When your church has an opportunity to hire, search for an individual that doesn't look like the majority race or gender in your church. Hire that person.

5) Listen to and value opinions of all people, no matter race, gender, nationality, or socioeconomic class. Remember the old adage, "hear before you are heard."

6) Use politics cautiously. According to Smith[35] the evangelical church is a stronghold of patriotism and nationalism. The church isn't the place to advocate for political ideologies.

7) Be real. Don't try to change your personality, including vocabulary, to reach individuals of other races, genders, nationalities, etc. True, we want our churches to look like Heaven but that won't occur through artificial means. Just embrace and love all people.

Despite our differences, we are all made in God's image. We all belong to God and should reflect God. Followers of Jesus are required—no exceptions—to embrace people from all backgrounds. Imagine what the crowd of saints are going to look like before God's throne? Will any groups be missing?

****

Priscilla and Aquilla were an early Church couple who, like Paul, were tentmakers. Paul stayed with them in Corinth and Ephesus, where the couple had churches in their home. After some time, Paul left Ephesus. Priscilla and Aquilla remained there. On a Sabbath morning in the Synagogue, Aquila and Priscilla heard a visitor, Apollos, speaking. Apollos was eloquent about the coming Messiah but knew only John's baptism of repentance.

Neither Priscilla nor Aquilla confronted Apollos in the Synagogue, nor attempted to embarrass Apollos by their superior knowledge of Jesus. Instead, they invited Apollos to their home, probably for a meal. They explained Jesus' life, finished work on the cross, and the baptism of the Holy Spirit. Their considerate approach added a strong voice to spread of the good news of Jesus.

Priscilla and Aquilla showed Christian love in their treatment of Paul and Apollos. When most 21st-century individuals think of love, they think of *eros*[5] which means erotic or passionate love. That type of love is the subject of books and movies galore. God's love is different. God's love is *agape*.[5] A Greek word, *agápe* means unconditional positive regard, acceptance, empathy, and universal love. *Agápe* is love for others that is based on our love of God and perhaps more importantly of God's love for us. *Agápe* is the love that Priscilla and Aquilla showed Apollos.

Where do you show agápe to others?

In the Acts of the early Christian church, Aquila and Priscilla are a stark contrast to Ananias and Sapphira. Ananias and Sapphira's love of prominence led to the first recorded sin in the new Christian church. Aquila and Priscilla modeled how a Christian couple shows love to others.

Below are two ways that ancient cultures failed to show love, alternating with how Christians showed love. In the ancient Roman Empire, infant girls were taken into the hills and left there. Animals ate them. Christians went into the hills and took female infants home to rear. In the Middle Ages, plagues occurred throughout Europe. Citizens who lived in towns fled to the countryside to avoid contact with contaminated individuals. Christians nursed plague-ridden individuals to wellness or to their deaths. Both groups acted out of love.

What about you—what are you doing in the 21st century out of love for individuals who are in difficult situations? Volunteering is an excellent way to show *agápe.* In my small city, we have homeless shelters that give individuals a place to stay at night and provide meals.

Another volunteer organization is Straight Street. It provides a positive Christian environment where at-risk youth can mature and discover God's divine plan for their lives. Lampstand is their human trafficking ministry that serves juvenile victims with support and a safe home.

Check out opportunities to share your love in your community by volunteering. There are more needs than volunteers and more needs than money.

If you're like me, about now you're saying, "Okay, now I know the definition of love, and I've seen how a loving person acts. But the truth is that on my own, I can't love another person as God loves me.

How do I become more loving?

As we open ourselves to the Holy Spirit increasing in us and our human nature decreasing, we become more loving. John the Apostle wrote that God's commandments aren't burdensome once we're saved (1 John 5:3-4), even his commandment to love our neighbor.

Love is an action. No, most of us will never be called upon to die for a brother or sister. Instead, John (1 John 3:17-18) recorded:

> If anyone has material possessions and sees a brother or sister in need but has no pity on them, how can the love of God be in that person? Dear children, let us not love with words or speech but with actions.

So what actions are you taking, or perhaps more importantly, going to take to show your love for God by showing your love for a neighbor?

Delving Deeper

Ligonier's Ministry[18] proposes that the gift of the Holy Spirit is the Holy Spirit. What does that mean? Do you agree or disagree?

Hebrews notes that we in the church must spur one another toward good deeds (Hebrews 10:24). List some ways you spur others on. Alternatively, list some ways you could spur others forward, but don't bother.

Why should race, gender, etc., not be the basis for Jesus being our Savior?

Paul wrote that love never fails. My love fails. Has yours? Identify a situation when your love failed? How can we ensure our love doesn't fail again?

The Bible's most famous chapter on love is 1 Corinthians 13. Read and ponder each verse in this chapter. Compare your thoughts and behavior to Paul's definition of love. Identify at least three differences.

Remember the famous rock song "All you need is love?" What do you need in addition to love to be a successful Jesus-follower?

CLOSING TIME

You finished this book. Finished means something has ended or concluded. I've completed what I set out to do—identify salient Bible episodes and show their meaning to 21st-century Christians. Many other Bible episodes could have been included. More of God's instructions on how to live our 21st-century lives could have been added. They weren't. I stopped writing this book.

Where should you go from here? The best place is in God's Word, the Bible. Read an episode from the Bible, then ponder it. Also, read what occurred before and after (this is context) the episode. Ask God to help you apply the episode's lessons to your life.

Take time to read other parts of the Bible that focus on the same topic. These related episodes and verses can help you expand your thoughts and subsequent actions. Have you heard the advice that the best way to interpret the Bible is through other Bible passages? Talk to your pastor or a seasoned Christian to validate what you learned and are thinking.

Make a list of things you want to change in your life based on episodes you've read. Take this step thoughtfully, praying continuously. Don't jump to a conclusion or aver to make a change too soon. Read the list every morning. Pray that God will assist you to make desired changes.

Hold yourself accountable for your list. One way to do that is to retrieve the list every evening. Re-read it. How did you do today? Where do you need more work to become more like Jesus? What items, behaviors, or actions are particularly hard for you? Talk to God about them. Identify an accountability partner to discuss your progress and challenges with.

In this book is one table (Table 1). I deliberately placed it after "Final Thoughts." Table 1 is subdivided into chapters and episodes, followed by the application topic for each episode. When you want a complete book reference, go to Table 1.

Table 1. Episodes & Applications

Ch	Episodes	Applications
1	*High Hopes*	
	Adam & Eve	Harmony, Equity
	Tree of Knowledge	Rebellion, Sin
	Consequences	Naked, Pain, Toil
	Tree of Life	Forfeiting life
	Noah	Refuge, Ridicule
2	*A New Day Has Come*	
	Abraham & Sarah	Aging
	Isaac & Abraham	Entanglements
	Jacob & Rebecca	Scheming
	Jacob & Rachel	Superstition/ Schemes
	Joseph	Favoritism
3	*Knockin on Heaven's Door*	
	Moses	Slander, Gossip
	Wood	Indestructible
	Curtains	Purity, Conceal
	Candlestick & Oil	Watch, Light
	Presence Bread	Gifts
4	*Promised Land*	
	Joshua	Accountability
	Deborah & Barak	Decision making
	Jael	Resourcefulness
	Jephthah	Rashness
	Naomi	Spiritual famine

Table 1. Episodes & Applications (cont'd)

Ch	Episodes	Applications
5	*Kings & Queens*	
	Saul	Exaltation
	David & Michal	Loneliness
	Solomon & Wives	Wisdom
	Divided Kingdom	Insults
	Queen Athaliah	Pride
6	*Freedom is a Voice*	
	Elijah & Jezebel	Persecution
	Isaiah's Poem	Discipline
	Hosea & Gomer	Idolatry
	Huldah	Anger
	Habakkuk	Complaints
	Zechariah	Hope
7	*Here Comes the Son*	
	Sermon on Mountain	Worry
	Parable of Bridesmaids	Preparation
	Prayer in Jesus' Life	Solitary
	Adulterous Woman	Judgment
	Miracle of Lazarus	Faith
8	*I See Clearly Now*	
	Holy Spirit	Helper
	Church	Jesus' Body
	Ananias & Sapphira	Lies
	Paul, Damascus road	Blindness
	Peter & Cornelius	Equity, Equality
	Priscilla & Aquilla	Love

CITATIONS

1. Van Heusen, Jimmy & Cahn, Sammy. 1959. "High Hopes." Genius. *https://genius.com.*

2. Lawrence, Brother. 2004. *The practice of the presence of God.* Henderson Christian Classics. *https:/christianbook.com.*

3. Nova, Aldo & Moccio, Stephan. 2002. "A New Day Has Come." Old Time Music. *https://oldtimemusic.com.*

4. Milton, John. n.d. Public Domain *Paradise Lost.*

5. Strong, James. 2010. *The new Strong exhaustive concordance of the Bible.* Nashville, TN: Thomas Nelson.

6. Festinger, Leon. 1962. A *Theory of Cognitive Dissonance.* Palo Alto: Stanford University Press.

7. Paul, Greg. 2018. 5 Ways Churches Play Favorites. Crosswalk.*https://crosswalk.com.*

8. Dylan, Bob. 1973. "Knockin on Heaven's Door." Song Facts. *https://songfacts.com.*

9. Shakespeare, William. 1623. Public Domain. *The Merchant of Venice.*

10. Berry, Chuck. 1965. "Promised Land." Old Time Music. *https//oldtimemusic.com.*

11. Kearney, Mat. 2022. "Kings & Queens." The Awesome Mix. *https://theawesomemix.com*

12. Boss, Jeff. 2015. 13 habits of humble people. *Forbes. https://forbes.com..*

13. Jeremiah, David. 2019. Three ways to overcome loneliness for Christians. *https://davidjeremiah.blog.*

14. "Jesus Walked This Lonesome Valley." Public Domain. *https://hymnary.org.*

15. Barber, Nigel. 2016. The psychology of insults. *Psychology Today.* *https://psychologytoday.com.*

16. Penny, Natasha. 2014. The fruits of pride. Hope Oak Church website. *https://hopeoakville.ca.*

17. McFerrin, Bobby. 2023." Freedom is Voice: The Meaning of Freedom is a Voice." Songtell. *https://songtell.com.*

18. Ligonier Ministry. 2024. Be angry, do not sin. Ligonier's Life Issues. *https://legoniers.org.*

19. Miles, Tracie. 2012. 7 ways to know when anger is a sin. Tracie Miles website. *https://traciemiles.com.*

20. Bloom, Jon. 2015. How to complain without grumbling. Desiring God website. *https://desiringGod.org.*

21. Mote, Edward. n.d. Public Domain. "My Hope is Built on Nothing Less." *https://myhymnary.org.*

22. Harrison, George. 1969. "Here Come the Sun." The Beatles Bible. *https://beatlesbible.com*

23. Carter, Joe. 2022. State of theology: What evangelicals believe in 2022. The Gospel Coalition. *https://thegospelcoalition.org.*

24. Macauthur, John. n.d. A worried Christian. Grace to You. *https://gty.org/library.*

25. Be Prepared: The Motto of the Boy Scouts of America. 1998. *Boy Scout Handbook.* *https://usscouts.org/usscouts/advance/boysc out/bsmotto.asp.* p. 54.

26. Mother Teresa of Calcutta. n.d. Mother Teresa's prayers. *https://slife.org/mother-teresas-prayers.*

27. Handel, Hiliary. 2022. Why we judge others and ourselves. *Psychology Today. https://psychologytoday.com.*

28. Barron, Kaelyn. n.d. How to be less judgmental. TCK Publishing. *https://tckpublishing.com.*

29. Piper, John. 2020. Miracles are meant to drive repentance. Desiring God website. *https://youtube.com.*

30. Nash, Johnny. 1972."The story of... I can see clearly now" Smooth Radio. *https://smoothradio.com.*

31. _____ Research reveals the most common reasons people lie. 2022. *Psychology Today. https.//psychologytoday.com.*

32. Brennan, Thomas. n.d. "Was blind but now I see." Bethlehem Church, Hampden, MA. *https://bethlehemhampdon.org.*

33. Newton, John. 1797. Public Domain. "Amazing grace." Timeless Truths. *https://library.timelesstruths.org.*

34. King, Martin Luther. 1963. Introduction. The King Center. *https://thekingcenter.org.*

35. Smith, Derek. 2022. Church diversity done right" Orange. *https://thinkorange.com.*

Carolyn A. Roth
Author

Carolyn is a spiritual woman who believes in the Trinity—God the Father, God the Son, and God the Holy Spirit. She believes that words in the Bible are God-inspired. She is an ordained minister.

Carolyn has advanced degrees in psychology and a doctorate from the University of San Francisco. She spent 25 years teaching in universities.

Carolyn is the author of several non-fiction books on the Bible. She is immersed in theology and science. She writes for the laity rather than clergy or theologians. Some of her books, like this one, are designed as Bible studies.

Contact Carolyn at carolyn.roth@ymail.com. Carolyn is eager to hear your questions and comments. The book is available on Amazon in paperback, electronic, and audio formats.